Praise for Michael E. Gerber
and *Beyond The E-Myth*

Michael's understanding of entrepreneurship and small business management has been a difference maker for countless businesses, including Infusion Software. His insights into the entrepreneurial process of building a business are a must-read for every small business owner. The vision, clarity, and leadership that came out of our Dreaming Room™ experience were just what our company needed to recognize our potential and motivate the whole company to achieve it.

—Clate Mask, president and CEO, Infusion Software

Everyone needs a mentor, someone who tells it like it is, holds you accountable, and shows you your good, bad, and ugly. For millions of small business owners, Michael Gerber is that person. Let Michael be your mentor and you are in for a kick in the pants, the ride of a lifetime.

—John Jantsch, author, *Duct Tape Marketing*

I was fortunate to meet Michael Gerber 20+ years ago when he helped teach me what it means to be a successful entrepreneur–clarify personal success and develop a Strategic Objective & Higher Purpose that is passionately aligned with your most powerful interests in life! This clarity has helped me find the required energy needed to do all the challenging things an entrepreneur needs to do to grow a successful and thriving business, while also enriching my life. He also helped me realize the extreme importance of marketing strategy and extraordinary systems, and how these two things can be so powerfully leveraged to create more life for all of an entrepreneur's stakeholders. Thank you Michael for all of your contributions to the field of entrepreneurial leadership, which continue to be deeply meaningful to me and those closest to me.

—Rob Siegfried, CEO & Founder of The Siegfried Group, LLP

Michael Gerber is an incredible business philosopher, guru, perhaps even a seer. He has an amazing intuition, which allows him to see in an instant what everybody else is missing; he sees opportunity everywhere. While in the Dreaming Room, Michael gave me the gift of seeing through the eyes of an awakened entrepreneur, and instantly my business changed from a regional success to serving clients on four continents.

—Keith G. Schiehl, President, Rent-a-Geek Computer Services

My heartfelt thank you, Michael, for taking me through your remarkable process of discovery. You've helped me understand that my business has nothing to do with me. You've opened my eyes to an often overlooked, critical fact: that a business does not produce a commodity to sell, rather it delivers an all-important service that meets the needs of its clients.

Your amazing vision has taken me to new heights that I otherwise could not have reached. You've stimulated me to think big. Well, not just big, but huge! No longer is my thinking restricted to my own limited reach. Now, thanks to your unique ability to inspire, I'm able to envision an enterprise that can serve the world!

Most importantly, I will always appreciate your authentic heart. Your passion for helping small business owners escape the calamitous fate most experience is absolutely incredible. You genuinely love people; and I can't think of a better attribute than that.

What better way to live life than to use your incredible talent in service of others; and it's for that I sincerely thank you!

—Chad Peshke, Financial Services Provider

*"For Everyone with a True Entrepreneurial Spirit
Who Wants to Make the Leap from a
'Small Business' to an 'Enterprise'"*

Beyond The E Myth

The Evolution of an Enterprise:

From a Company of One
to a Company of 1,000!

MICHAEL E. GERBER

Published by
Prodigy Business Books, Inc., Carlsbad, California.

Production Team
Trish Beaulieu, COO, Prodigy Business Books, Inc.; Larry Heiman, editor; Marilyn Geary, proofreader; Nancy Ratkiewich, cover design and book production, njr productions; Jeff Kassebaum, Michael E. Gerber author photographer, Jeff Kassebaum and Co.

For general information on other products and services, please visit the website: www.michaelegerbercompanies.com.

ISBN 978-1-61835-048-0 (cloth)
ISBN 978-1-61835-049-7 (audio)
ISBN 978-1-61835-039-8 (ebook)

Printed in the United States of America

10 9 8 7 6 5 4 3 2 1

To Luz Delia, my champion, my partner,

my indefatigable warrior, lover of the truth,

student of the divine, wife, friend, joyous

creator, everything I do is for you . . .

—Michael E. Gerber

Table of Contents

PART II

PART III

PART IV

PART V

ACKNOWLEDGMENTS

It is literally impossible to acknowledge everyone who has made such a significant contribution to the 40-year journey I've undergone in my E-Myth enterprise as those who follow, but allow me to try:

To all the **E-Myth coaches,** past present and future, your resilience, dedication to your clients, and your generosity of spirit as we worked our way through the sometimes glacial obstacles we faced, thank you from the bottom of my heart, especially to my most recent: **Remy Gervais, Larry Heiman,** and **Joe Wollenweber,** taking these most precious steps forward with *Beyond The E-Myth* couldn't have happened without you.

To **Larry Heiman,** for your brilliant and tempestuous editing of this book, what a storm of impossibilities you were confronted with, what a noble confrontation you made with those impossibilities . . . many more books to do, many more impossibilities to overcome.

To **Trish Beaulieu,** partner, chief collaborator, great friend and determined always to get everything right, even those things which never could be, you will see this enterprise to its worthy end, thank you for your gifts of caring, and your signature warmly.

To **Nancy Ratkiewich,** how you manage to persist despite all of the late nights, impossible objectives, changes of mind incessantly, how you keep up with it and us so magnificently as you do is beyond me.

To **Dave Jenyns,** our book launch master, without whom this book would never have seen the light of day, a late arrival, but such an essential one, so much more to do together as our enterprise sees the light of day.

To **Jamie Gilleland,** wow, such a glad and rewarding gift you've become, with love and a strong shoulder, never allowing anything to drop even when there was more to carry than an ordinary person could, you are our love, our friend, our outreach invincible.

To **Chris Goegan,** how many times do we need to say it, how many times have we, your golden aura, illimitable smile, your conviction about great standards, and your friendship beneath it all, thank you.

To **Hal Coffin,** the only word that best describes you is steadfast, which is the contribution you've continually and tirelessly and warmly and intelligently made to our lives, our venture, the work you've so tirelessly devoted yourself to, every company should be so fortunate to have the financial tower you've become for us, thank you dear friend for your generosity of love and spirit.

When it comes to knowing my voice and being it, **Marilyn Geary** has been at my side and in my mind for more years than either of us would care to remember! Thank you dear Marilyn, for your persistence, your patience, your deep and gracious understanding.

Yes, like each of you, I've got a life to live, which includes everything I've got to go through just to handle it. For years, **Aurika Fedun** has made certain I'm cared for. Thank you, Aurika, I have absolutely no idea how you manage it all, with such kind and wondrous attention to all the detail!

And, if the money doesn't work, what then? You guessed it: chaos! Our **Jaqi Beasley** is the one who keeps us sane, all our books in balance, and, wonder of wonders, without losing her own. Thank you, kind Jaqi. You're our personal gold mine, a pure treasure we could never live without!

And to the Infusionsoft colleagues, the 1-800 Got Junk folks, and our very own Vertical Experts and Co-Authors, without you my Dreams would continue to be just that.

And then there's **Rodger Ford,** the man who I met over an artificial heart, the remarkable product of just one of his many equally remarkable enterprises, a scion of the original, the most resourceful CEO, Founder and Entrepreneur I've ever met, thank you so much, Rodger, for your continued enthusiasm for my work, my continuously accelerating plans, my extravagant imagination, and for your prodigiously ironic Reliant Heart, my world would not be even close to the same without you . . .

WWW.BEYONDEMYTH.COM   PAGE | iii

ABOUT THIS BOOK

The Universally Applicable Hierarchy of Growth

If you own a small business, and if your business depends upon you to survive, it's what I call "a Company of One."

Which means, that the vast majority of small businesses are a Company of One.

Which means, this book was written for you.

It is a simple, yet provocative, formula for re-designing, re-building, re-launching, and exponentially re-growing what you currently think of as your small business, but which, in reality, is not a business at all.

What is it then, if it is not a business?

Why a job, of course.

A job for you.

This book is going to turn your thinking about your job into a stunning enterprise. You might ask: "What's the difference between the two?"

The difference between night and day.

But don't take my word for it. Just settle down and read it straight through.

It's short, it's sweet, and it's intended to transform the state of your "Company of One" into a "Company of One Thousand," not, however, by telling you HOW to do it, but much more importantly, by telling you exactly WHAT must be done, and WHY.

Over the 40 years I've been immersed in the field of small business, it perpetually surprises me how illogically most of those I've met approached the process for designing, building, launching, and growing a "Great Growing Company."

Indeed, if one were to believe the stories told and advice given, you would walk away with the conclusion that every business is different, ergo unique, and that every process for growing every business must be different as well.

This flies in the face of my conclusion, which is that every company—though absolutely unique in its own identifiable way—is in critical and fundamental form and function the same as every other company. Therefore, the process of business development for each company is identical from one to the other. This has proven itself to be transformational. And our successes at applying that logic—in every kind of company, in every kind of Industry worldwide—are legion.

This book shares that exact process with you, my reader, in order to, once and for all, simplify it, clarify it, and thereby eliminate the immense confusion that exists out there in the world of small business development.

So, the accumulated experiences of 40 years are compiled and consolidated here for you, all for the purpose of realizing my life-long goal of creating the economic revolution that cannot help but occur when good minds, pure intentions, and proven practices intersect to permanently transform the state of small business worldwide.

To you, and to your application of what is shared here, I wish you great traveling—as a grand level of growth and your legacy are to follow!

Warmly,

Michael E. Gerber
Chairman and Co-Founder
Chief Dreamer
Michael E. Gerber Companies, Inc.™

PREFACE

I will not learn about fire by thinking about fire but by burning.
—Carla Needleman, *From The Work of Craft*

This is the simplest book I've ever written.

It's a book written for everyone who has started his own business, or for everyone who hopes to.

It's a simple book because it starts out with a simple premise. That unless you start your business with the intention of selling it, it will almost always turn out to be a disaster.

So this book is about going to work ON your business (I'm going to call it a "company" from now on), to design your company, to build your company, to launch your company, and then to grow your company for the extreme purpose of preparing your company for sale.

That means that a company, no matter what it does, and how it does that, is nothing other than a product. A product you're preparing for sale.

After all is said and done, that's what an entrepreneur is: an inventor of a grand and growing company—a product–which ultimately will be sold to a buyer who falls madly in love with it.

Every company on the face of the planet is nothing other than a product for sale.

But, the buyer of your company, whomever that may be, doesn't fall in love with what the company *does;* he's much more pragmatic than that. The buyer falls in love with how *well* your company does it.

And the measure for how well a company does what it does is only two things: first, its success in its ability to attract and keep customers better than any other company; and second, the return on equity a company produces time after time after time.

In sum, such a company–a company which buyers absolutely love—possesses the uncanny, and seemingly unnatural, ability to scale.

Which, put in a much simpler way, is that company's intuitively brilliant ability to grow.

GREAT COMPANIES GROW GREATLY

Great growing companies know how to replicate their success, time after time after time. And by doing so, they grow, grow, grow.

This book is going to teach you how to do that.

This book is going to teach you how to design, build, launch, and grow your company so that it can scale. Which means it can replicate its success. Which means it possesses the ability to grow like crazy, or as we put it in the title of this book, "From a Company of One, to a Company of 1,000!"

Which means it's a Great Growing Company!

The vast majority of small companies on the planet–incorrectly called "small businesses" (you'll understand the distinction as you read further in this book), are a fool's errand.

Because very, very few of those fool's errands, those very small companies, were built on the premise I'm going to be sharing with you in this book: that Job #1 of a small company's owner is . . . to prepare his or her company for sale.

Which means to focus on equity, rather than on income.

To start a small company with anything else as your focus is a fool's errand.

But take heart!

This book can be used to turn those fool's errands completely around.

To turn them into something remarkably other than a fool's errand.

To turn them from a bogged down, solipsistic company of one, to an absolutely brilliant enterprise of 1,000!

NO SCALE, NO SALE

That's the key to what I'm going to be sharing with you here. No scale, no sale.

A great buddy of mine, Rodger Ford, serial founder and remarkably brilliant "imagineer" (as Walt Disney would put it) of many great growing companies over his illustrious entrepreneurial career put it this way:

> *I have been responsible for several business successes including AlphaGraphics, PetsHotel, SynCardia and ReliantHeart.*
>
> *At every turn in the road or opportunity to make improvement, Michael E. Gerber was there by my side. You might say he was whispering in my ear. Encouraging me to evaluate the exception and hardscape solutions so that ordinary people can continue to experience extraordinary success.*
>
> *It is the routine in business that liberates the individuals within the business to best serve the customer. And the modern electronic communication and documentation tools of today create the platform to further embrace the philosophy of Michael as elegantly taught by* The E-Myth.
>
> *—Rodger Ford, CEO, ReliantHeart, Inc.*

Which means that at the very heart of this book echoes my original E-Myth mantra: "Go to work ON your business, not just IN your business."

This is the mantra Rodger applied in every one of his companies.

But what does that really mean?

It means that your job as a founder, a grower, an inventor, an innovator, is to design, build, launch, and grow your small company so that it possesses the ability to do exactly what McDonald's was designed to do: deliver identically the same, uniquely branded McDonald's products, again and again and again, in the hands of kids at minimum wage, despite their seemingly impossible 300% annual personnel turnover. And then, once so built, to unapologetically, unabashedly—faithfully—scale it to grow.

That means to produce tens of thousands of stores worldwide. Each and every one of those stores doing identically the very same thing, time after time after time, in the very same way.

Just like a Big Mac is made, just so is the company that makes that Big Mac made.

When you can do that in *your* company—and in this book I'm saying that you *must* do that—there's a buyer waiting, ready, willing and able to buy your company for the price you're determined to get for it.

Not just one buyer, but dozens upon dozens of buyers.

And I'm not talking about the "billions of buyers served here," like McDonald's says and does.

No, that's not the buyer we're talking about here.

The buyer we're talking about here is the buyer of your company!

The reason there are dozens and dozens and dozens of buyers for the business called McDonald's is because there are billions and billions served, and countless billions more!

And those buyers of the company called McDonald's are buying it every single day, even as you're reading this, in the form of McDonald's stock.

There's no getting around it, the public company called McDonald's is a product for sale.

And that was the intent from the outset. There at the drawing board of the tiny McDonald's corporation, way back in the '50s. Way back in the '50s when they were lining up to buy the company called McDonald's after the 50-plus-year-old Ray Kroc crafted his very first store—his franchise prototype—the intent was to scale for sale.

And the franchisees bought it.

And they bought it for the very same reason everyone else was buying it.

Because McDonald's was designed, built, launched, and grown in exactly the way I'm going to share with you here.

From a tiny hamburger stand—a company of one—to a stunningly immense enterprise; a company of (exponentially more than) 1,000–step by step by step by irresistibly replicatable step.

"The System runs the business," Ray Kroc said, "and the people run the System!"

That's exactly what you get to do. Ready your company for sale. Just like Ray Kroc did, starting out at the age of 52!

If, that is, you're up to it.

Let's see if you are.

WHAT IT TAKES TO GROW A COMPANY OF ONE TO A COMPANY OF 1,000!

Well, first of all, it takes passion. Unbridled passion. Which means you can feel the unquenchable heat of it all day long. From the moment you get up, till the moment you try to go to sleep, but can't. Burning with the question: "What's missing in this picture?"

In short, you've got to be *inspirable*. From the inside and the outside. You've got to be more than just open to the question, "what would that take?" You've got to be able to leave all of your excuses behind. Your yes, buts. Your precious reasons for being who you are, where you are, doing what you do, the way you do. Leave behind your well-trod excuse for being far less than you could be. You've got to be really far past just curious about the proposition that someone can take a company of one and turn it into a company of 1,000. You've got to be blown away by it! You've got to be the kind of person who opens the front door without asking, "Who's there?"

Second, you've got to be instructable.

Meaning, you'll sit down in this class and take notes. Copious notes. And before you rush to ask a question, you'll listen instead to the answer I'm giving you, which, you'll discover throughout this book, will almost always sound like a question rather than an answer. So, you've got to be a really good student. Knowing even as you start this conversation with me that you're completely incapable of understanding what I'm intending to teach you. Primarily because you've never DONE what I'm intending to teach you. So, this book, and what follows it, is going to be like walking on a new planet. The new planet called exponential growth. And despite what you may think about growth, it's nothing like what you think it is. Yes, you've got to be irresistibly instructable. And, don't forget . . . *passionate*. Which means, *resolute*. Which means, *indefatigable*.

Third, you've got to accept the stubborn fact that this process can only be taken one step at a time.

You can't rush it.

There are no leap-overs in this process.

First this, then that, is the rule of the day.

I will, of course, explain exactly what "this" is even before I ask you to take that step; but still, and mostly, you're going to be completely in the dark every step of the way.

And that's the way it's supposed to be.

Because if you weren't in the dark, you wouldn't feel the need to find the light, would you?

And without the need to find the light there can be no progress, can there?

So you're going to simply have to trust me when I say that each and every step will absolutely take you from dark to light.

And that each new step into the light will also take you to a greater light than the one before it.

So much so that you're going to be continuously experiencing that the light you thought you experienced, was, in relationship to the very next step, actually dark.

Which means that at each iterative step what you believe to be true is actually only an indicator of the truth you're about to discover.

And that process will continually repeat itself.

Provided, that is, you've got what it takes.

Remember, the ultimate sale of your company is the end game here.

So, finally, you've got to be committed to stay with it.

No matter what.

You've got to be a stayer if you're going to be a player.

Because this journey is going to be challenging you every single step of the way.

And frustrating you. And pissing you off.

Because you're going to be failing far more often than winning.

And I know this all sounds like a great big cliché.

But it sounds that way, because it is a cliché.

But, when you think about it, *everything* is a cliché, isn't it?

That is, until you live it.

When you live the process I'm going to be introducing you to here, you'll find that every word describing it: frustration, failure, success, inspiration and so forth, have all been endlessly written about—and experienced— millions upon millions of times before you experience them.

But, when you experience them, they cease being clichés.

They're what's called instead, life.

Life is a cliché when you come right down to it.

But not to the person *living* it.

So, you've got to be a stayer, no matter what happens along the way.

We're here to prepare your company for sale.

That's the only reason we're here.

Are you up to it?

Well, then. Let's get started.

Let's take a leap *Beyond The E-Myth*.

INTRODUCTION

If you're going to design, build, launch, and grow your company to prepare it for sale, there must be a clear process for doing it. I call it *Beyond The E-Myth,* because while *The E-Myth,* my very first book, and its cohort, *The E-Myth Revisited,* provide the necessary point of view in order to organize the way you THINK about being a business owner, they don't provide you with the mindset needed to focus your attention on how to prepare your company for that singular, life-transforming event—your Liquidity Date, your Exit Strategy, the day, God willing, the Big Sale happens.

That's the purpose of this book.

I call it *Beyond The E-Myth,* because that's literally the "Sole Purpose" of what we're about to do, going beyond The E-Myth to make absolutely certain that in order to achieve that singular objective—your Liquidity Date—you put on the hat of a great entrepreneur . . . and never take it off!

"Sole Purpose" is critical here.

"Sole Purpose" is to design, build, launch, and grow your company in exactly and definitively the way it must be done in order to prepare it for that supreme moment when the prospective buyer of your company, whoever that may be, walks in your door and asks you to show her your company, and you not only can, but in precisely the way that will assure you she will say, "Yes!"—*with a great big check!*

But, as most small business owners and entrepreneurs know, this is not so easily done.

"Wants to understand," is a key phrase in all this.

Your prospective buyer wants to understand. Wants to understand what your company does, how your company does it, why your company does what it does, and what its Great and Singular Purpose is for being the company that it is, all while fighting to hear you above the noise of the ever-increasingly complicated and dysfunctional world of "businesses" out there on the streets, both competing with you and competing for your buyer's attention.

And it makes absolutely no difference to your potential buyer whether those streets are virtual or brick and mortar; she's up for anything that works better than everyone else's, provided there's a big and bodacious market for it, that is.

"Show me," she's going to say. And show her you must. But what you show her, and how you show it to her is the ball game here.

This book is about exactly that: what you're going to show her, and how.

But for us to achieve our Sole Purpose here, this book must be much more than just that.

In order to get at that indelible moment when you're going to parade your prized company out for inspection, we need to walk you through the process of creating that Great Growing Company you're setting out to create.

And at the outset—because that's where we are right now—in that you haven't got a Great Growing Company at all right now, you're going to set out to create one with what I call *"a blank piece of paper and beginner's mind."*

Meaning, to first envision that great growing enterprise, your very first step is what I have named "The Dreaming Room." Think of this as the incubator where your Dream, your Vision, your Purpose, and your Mission are awakened in your Dreamer's, your Thinker's, your Storyteller's, and your Leader's mind. You must first see what you're about to create, if you are ever going to be able to actually create it. And, of course, both must happen if you are ever going to be able to sell it.

So, let's walk through what you're going to find in this book. The nuts and bolts of it, so to speak.

The Nuts and Bolts of It

To set the stage for what you're about to do, it's important to face the reality of the marketplace, the marketplace of "small business"—what it looks like, why it looks like it does, and why that's extremely important for the conversation we're about to have.

Because the marketplace of small business is where your competition lives.

Not just the competition for the business you're in, the products or services you intend to sell, and how you manage to do all that, but the competition for the <u>business</u> you're ultimately intending to *sell*.

You can't but be aware that there is a whole slew of companies who are determined to take your customers away; and that's a battle you're going to have to be prepared to fight if you're ever going to survive to the point of the ultimate sale of your company.

But, the true competition comes at the end of the game, not at the beginning of it.

The true competition really kicks in when you want to sell your company.

That's the ice-water-in-the-face time for most business owners.

That's the "holy shit" moment when most—say about 99%—of all companies wake up to the realization that they've been doing it all wrong.

All of that hard work, all of that great suffering, all of that "doing it, doing it, doing it" that they've been consumed with during the years preceding that moment when they finally think to themselves: "How do I get the hell out of here? How do I sell it?"

Then and only then do they come to see that there is no way they're going to get the hell out of there. There is no way they're going to sell it.

Because there is no one, absolutely no one, who wants to buy it!

That's the tragic truth of this tale.

Most small companies will *never* be sold.

And they'll never be sold because the only person who might consider buying one of them is really only looking for a job. And that guy doesn't have any money!

An accountant is looking for an accounting practice.

A chiropractor is looking for a chiropractic practice.

A poodle clipper is looking for a poodle clipping practice.

And if that erstwhile buyer, who, in reality, is a job seeker wanting to be his own boss, doesn't have any money, what's that seller going to do when that buyer is gone?

You got it. He just ekes out the rest of his life until he closes his business. And then goes into subsistence. On Medicare. Collecting Social Security, supplemented by whatever he may have managed to save over those hard years. "Doing it, doing it, doing it" some more, whatever that looks like. Whatever that means.

Yes, the sad and tragic story of most small business owners when their business comes to a close is that . . . *so does their life!*

Wow! Is that what you're doing this all for?

Well, of course it isn't.

But, that's exactly what's going to happen if you ignore what I'm going to share with you here.

That's the sad and sorry reality of the small business marketplace.

That is the true nuts and bolts of it.

Design your company for sale, or suck wind when you're done. Exactly at the time you can least afford to!

THE EVOLUTION OF AN ENTERPRISE

Which is why in this book I'm starting out at the very beginning of your company, where you're standing right now.

What I call NewCo, rather than OldCo.

Because unless we start out at the very beginning of this company you're designing for eventual sale, at NewCo rather than at OldCo, we'll hopelessly be called to *fix* OldCo, trying to make it work better than it does, and while that's what everybody tries to do, it's the very worst strategy of all.

So, instead of applying my working ON it mantra to OldCo, as everyone thinks they need to do, we're going to apply it instead to the company I call NewCo, by asking you the most essential questions anyone can ask of the company you're about to create: "What is it here to do, and why?"

Or, said in another way: "What's your company's Dream, Vision, Purpose, and Mission?"

Your **Dream** is the great result your company intends to produce.

Your **Vision** is the form your company must take in order to produce that result.

Your **Purpose** is the outcome you're going to produce for your most important customer.

Your **Mission** is the core operating system you must invent for your company to succeed at what it's setting out to do.

DREAMING THE E-MYTH:

*In my case, early on in my entrepreneurial career, way back then in 1977, my **Dream** was "to transform the state of small business worldwide."*

*My **Vision** was "to invent the McDonald's of small business consulting."*

*My **Purpose** was to make it possible for every independently owned small business owner who heeded our call to create a small* company as successful and as replicable as a McDonald's franchise was and is.

My **Mission** was to invent a turnkey, intelligent, business development system we could deliver to every small business owner in every vertical market—chiropractors, physicians, contractors, gas stations, coffee shops, attorneys, you name it—at less than the cost of a minimum wage employee.

Turnkey consulting.

Just like McDonald's was and is.

Deliverable by anyone, regardless of their personal level of business experience.

And that's what we knew had to be done in order to prepare our company for sale.

And, no, I didn't set out to become a great consultant or coach.

I set out instead to create a great consulting **system** that, once done, once proven successful, once it worked everywhere we were called to apply it, would be eminently scalable.

And because of that, we would transform an industry that hadn't yet begun.

In short, we created the coaching industry.

Eleven billion dollars strong today.

And we did that by coming to grips with what I *now* call "the evolution of an enterprise."

And that progression is the roadmap and the key to the eventual sale of your company.

Because unless and until you can do that very same thing for your customer—meaning your company—there will be no Exit Strategy for you or your family.

There will be no Liquidity Date.

There will be no great buyer at your door.

There will be only more of the same.

Let's not let that happen.

Let's flesh out the rest of this story, so you can completely understand what we're about to do together, and why.

Your Buyer Is Looking for Scale

Your buyer isn't looking for the company you are today. Your buyer is looking for the company you'll become in the future.

Because that's where your buyer will find HIS Exit Strategy.

Whether that's going public, or being acquired, or growing it like crazy, as Facebook has done.

The ability to scale is the key to all that.

And unless your company can demonstrate that it possesses the ability to scale, to grow, grow, grow, because the way it does what it does is truly scalable, your buyer won't become your buyer, he'll not even say, "hello"!

So, let's look at the process for scale.

THE DREAMING ROOM: THE PLATFORM FOR EXPONENTIAL GROWTH

The first step, as I've already said, is your Dream, your Vision, your Purpose, and your Mission—the ever-loving platform for exponential growth.

Your **Dream** tells the story of who you intend to become. The Great Result your company intends to produce in a way no other company has ever produced it.

Your **Vision** tells the story of what your company will look like, act like, and be like in order to manifest that dream as an ongoing reality. That's why I said, "to become the McDonald's of small business consulting." Because IF we could do that, we then would have achieved the strategic result every sensible buyer would be passionate about. Why? Because McDonald's is the most successful small business in the world! What an exemplary model to fashion our great company on. And it was never a question of IF we could do that. It was simply a question of HOW we would do that. That's what we set out to do. And that's what I'm suggesting that YOU must set out to do, no matter what kind of business you're in.

Your **Purpose** tells the singular story of why your company is worth doing. It's all about your most important customer. Who they are, why they are, and what's going on with them. Your Purpose starts and ends with your most important customer. Just as at E-Myth, our Dream said our most important customer was an independently owned small business. Or, rather the owner of one. And there were millions of them. Billions, actually, worldwide. All of them struggling to get by. None of them truly understanding why it's such a struggle. What if we could figure that out for them? That was our purpose. To figure that out for them. To figure out why most small businesses don't work and what to do about it. Which is the subtitle of my most famous book, *The E-Myth*. Get it? That's what you've got to do as well. Figure it out for them. For your most important customer. And then, once you get that that's what you as a newly born entrepreneur are here to do, you'll then, perhaps for the very first time, understand that unless or until you do that, you'll never succeed at selling it. Not to Microsoft. Not to Apple. Not to Mary Kay Cosmetics. Not to Google. Not to anyone who is a truly spectacular buyer of small, scalable companies . . . in order to better grow theirs! Because you won't have a worthwhile story to tell them.

And, finally, your **Mission** will show your most important buyer how you did what you set out to do. Your Mission is the system at the heart of it all. Just like the system is at the heart of McDonald's. Just like the system is at the heart of Mary Kay Cosmetics. Just like the system is at the heart of Starbucks, and Subway, and Apple, and Ameriprise, and Century 21, and UPS, and Uber, and so forth and so forth and so forth. It's "the System, Stupid!" is what everyone knows it must be. Because without a proprietary, turnkey, scalable, muscular, indigenous and intelligent system at the heart of YOUR company, it will never be able to do what the word "scalable" demands it to do. In short, without that remarkably sonorous system living and breathing at the heart of your company, without that turnkey operating system—the OS of your business—there will never be a brand worthy of that name. There will never be a personality great gobs of customers identify with. As they do with Apple. As they do with Starbucks. As they do with every Great Growing Company worthy of the name. There will never be what's needed to make your sale.

So, you see, how you *start* NewCo will determine how you *end* NewCo.

Yes, you must consider the exit from the very beginning. It is easy to start a company. It is difficult to sell a company. If you don't consider your Exit Strategy from the beginning, you are simply creating a job for yourself. A job you can't quit because you're the boss.

And that's why "a blank piece of paper and beginner's mind" are so critical at this stage of the game.

Because, without them there is no basis for a foundational strategy.

And without a foundational strategy, all we've got left is "doing it, doing it, doing it!"

Which is the tactical reality of almost every small company.

Let's grow beyond that.

THE HIERARCHY OF CONTINUOUS GROWTH

So, you've now got your platform for exponential growth in place.

You've got your Dream, Vision, Purpose, and Mission well in hand.

What's next?

What's next is putting your platform to work. And the way you put your platform to work is by taking your company through the evolution we've spoken about before.

Think of it as "the hierarchy of continuous growth."

After you've created the platform, the very next step in the hierarchy of growth is called **The Job.**

The Job is not the job every small business owner does. It's not the "doing it, doing it, doing it" version of the job we're all so self-consciously familiar with.

The Job we're talking about here is the creation of your turnkey <u>Client Fulfillment System</u>.

Without that, there will never be a scalable company.

It all begins or dies right here.

This choice to invent your Client Fulfillment System is the most elemental entrepreneurial choice of them all.

If you fail to make that choice, or, even worse, make the wrong choice, (as most small business owners continue to do), its Medicaid and Social Security without fail. It's "doing it, doing it, doing it" until you simply can't do it anymore.

So, really, step one of *Beyond The E-Myth* is making the sure decision that your job, your most *important* job as a new entrepreneur, is to *decide* at the very beginning, right here, right now, that you're in it for only one reason: to get your company ready for sale.

And the invention of your Client Fulfillment System is where you begin.

Which is Step Two.

THE JOB: YOUR CLIENT FULFILLMENT SYSTEM

Your Client Fulfillment System is the methodology through which you deliver the result you have promised to deliver to your most important customer in your Dream, Vision, Purpose, and Mission.

It's the how you do what you intend to do that's most critical to building the core, intrinsic value underlying the ultimate value of your company.

The Job, then, is a visual Job, an emotional Job, a functional Job, and a financial Job.

It's how you integrate the visual, emotional, functional and financial components of your company of one as you design, build, launch, and grow it to become a company of 1,000.

So, it starts here at the very beginning with your NewCo.

At The Job.

And this is critical to understand: Rather than doing what most people will insist you need to do, i.e. focus your attention on getting customers—on sales–your first job in creating The Job has *nothing to do with sales*. It has everything to do with Client Fulfillment. That is the core operating system behind what your company is solely here to do. At the heart of what you intend to do is the system that defines, controls, and delivers everything you intend your client to experience from your company.

Call it the "QuickBooks" of your company. The operating system which enables you to touch your most important customer to the quick.

Not that it IS software—at least not in the way we think of when we say the word software.

But like software (which is simply a coded system designed to support a particular set of results), your Client Fulfillment System—which may be or include software—is the method through which you produce the result your company was designed to produce for your customer.

THE JOB OF THE E-MYTH EXPERIENCE:

In my case, way back in 1977, it was (and still is) the method through which we taught small business owners how to THINK about business, the core operating reality of any small business . . . what we named "The Seven Centers of Management Attention."

Nobody, not Peter Drucker, not Theodore Levitt, not any of the thought leaders of business back then, had ever organized the mindset about business in the way we set out to do.

We set out to invent what we called the "franchise prototype" paradigm—the business model I created for building a truly spectacular small business to grow.

That entire system—that way of thinking–made it possible for us to organize the key components of what began in 1977 as The Michael Thomas Business Development Program and, after my first book was written, became The E-Myth Mastery Program.

Today, it has evolved into what you're holding in your hands right now: Beyond The E-Myth—The Evolution of an Enterprise: From a Company of One to a Company of 1,000!

A System is a way of thinking. And then, provided that that way of thinking has legs, it is a way of doing. And provided that way of doing has legs, a way of growing. And provided that way of growing has legs, a way of being acquired.

So, here we are at the very beginning of that process. Evolving.

This is the beginning where you have imagined, created, captured, and codified your uniquely profound way of attracting and transforming the mindset of your most important customer, and by so doing, transforming the way they live their lives, like McDonald's did. Like FedEx did. Like, well you get it. Like every stunningly inventive great growing enterprise does.

So, now that you've invented your turnkey Client Fulfillment System, and documented it in manuals, your software, your "This is how we do it here!" book, we can go on to Step Three. The Practice. Your <u>Client Acquisition System</u>.

The Practice: Your Client Acquisition System

You know what you're here to sell.

You have documented it and put it into your "This is how we do it here!" book–which is the most important book you will ever write in your life, because you can transfer it to someone other than yourself.

And now you're ready for Step Three. The Practice. And it is actually two legs of what I call your "three-legged stool."

Your Practice is your Franchise Prototype.

It's the core operating system of your company for growth.

The first leg of your Franchise Prototype is the leg you've just invented and built, your Client Fulfillment System.

The second leg of your Franchise Prototype is called Lead Generation.

The third leg of your Franchise Prototype is called Lead Conversion.

Put those last two legs together—Lead Generation and Lead Conversion— and you have your Client Acquisition System.

Put the three legs together, and you have the very heart of your about-to-be-developed, business operating system—the franchise you're about to grow.

WHY "FRANCHISE"?

Over the years, our use of this word "franchise" has been a sticky notion to some. It needn't be. It should, in fact, be totally liberating. It should provide a unifying guideline to any entrepreneur intending to grow from one to 1,000. Let me clarify so that it doesn't stand in the way, but rather, lights the way:

Think of the word "franchise" any way you like. Think of it literally, that you're actually going to franchise your company, creating multiple copies, over and over and over again. Or, think of it metaphorically, that you're not actually going to franchise it, but you are going to grow it exponentially, systematically and systemically, in whatever form you've decided it will take.

But, however you think of the word "franchise," understand that at its essence it is simply the unique, sustainable, and growable value of a business. And understand that the process of growth can be no better implemented than by thinking of it through that lens. Because you are a franchisor, whether you think that way or not.

In that way, Apple is a franchise, as is Google, as is every company on the face of the planet, if they're humongously successful, that is.

When you strip it down to the bones, a "franchise" is quite simply your company's proprietary way of doing what it does. It is the unique way you do that, captured in your operating system, and available to everyone who needs to know, so that they can do it exactly as you dreamed it—so it can be flawlessly scaled.

Because the word "scale" lives at the heart of every great company. And there's only one way to do that. And that one way to achieve that one way is what I'm introducing to you right here.

Which is how you create a great Business.

THE BUSINESS: AND YOUR TURNKEY MANAGEMENT SYSTEM

There was a reason why you designed, built, launched, and then grew your turnkey Practice, and then documented it.

Because without doing that you could never grow a Business.

So, let's make sure you understand this hierarchy:

Your Business is the aggregate of up to <u>seven turnkey Practices</u>, driven by a turnkey Management System.

Practice Number One is an aggregate of your <u>Lead Generation, Lead Conversion</u>, and <u>Client Fulfillment Systems</u>: Your three-legged stool.

Practice Number Two is the very same thing.

Practice Number Three is as well, as are Practices Four, Five, Six, and Seven.

When you achieve up to seven Practices, they together constitute a Business.

Why seven?

Because it is almost impossible to effectively manage eight.

And if we're going to grow it exponentially, we've got to be able to manage it exponentially.

Imagine your Client Fulfillment System as the hub of your Business Wheel, with your seven Practices as the seven spokes.

Imagine your turnkey Management System as the software at the hub of your Business Wheel, enabling and powering each and every one of your people, whatever their role is on that wheel—Lead Generation, Lead Conversion, Client Fulfillment— to access exactly what each needs to know in order to perform what they're responsible for in the implementation of their turnkey responsibility.

A Business

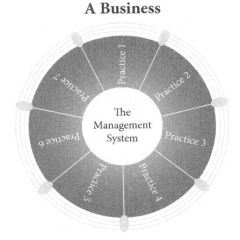

In truth, your Business cannot operate effectively without this matrix!

And if your Business cannot operate effectively without it, it can't grow!

And the entire purpose of all this is to prepare and then enable your company to grow. From a Company of One, to a Company of 1,000!

Which then prepares it to design, build, launch, and grow your exhilarating Enterprise!

Ambitious? Well, of course. This entire mindset is ambitious. And if it weren't ambitious it wouldn't be entrepreneurial.

What else is an entrepreneur if not ambitious?

That's why the term "solopreneur" is a contradiction in terms.

True Entrepreneurs *never* go solo!

True Entrepreneurs grow a Great Growing Company.

And unless it becomes a Great Growing Company, it's not ever going to be sold.

Because that's all the buyer wants.

Remember, the buyer is buying the future, not the past.

Your systems and foundation infuse the buyer with confidence in what he is buying and provide the platform from which all improvement flows.

And that's why we've been doing all this work on The Job, on The Practice, and now, on he Business.

Getting it ready for sale.

THE ENTERPRISE: AND YOUR TURNKEY LEADERSHIP SYSTEM

Your Enterprise is the end product of this entire process. It is the product of the hierarchy of growth. It's the reason we'll been doing this work together. It's the "Enterprise" we're speaking about in "The Evolution of an Enterprise." And it's why we're talking about "companies" and not "small businesses," because, as you can now see, they're not "businesses" at all.

Because if they were "businesses," they would only be "businesses" in order to design, build, launch, and grow into an enterprise, which is the culmination of the business development process we're engaged in here.

And the sole reason for that is to design a business product for someone—an investor, a buyer, a strategic partner, a Great Growing Company of its own—to acquire.

So, let's then define an Enterprise in much the same way as we defined a Business.

An **Enterprise** is an aggregate of up to <u>seven turnkey Businesses</u>, plus a <u>turnkey Leadership System</u>.

See the seven turnkey Businesses, again, in much the same way as we saw them earlier, as an aggregate of up to seven turnkey Practices.

Business Number One comprises up to seven turnkey Practices, each of which comprises a turnkey Lead Generation System, a turnkey Lead Conversion System, and a turnkey Client Fulfillment System.

As do Businesses Numbers Two, Three, Four, Five, Six, and Seven.

So, our Enterprise, comprising as it does up to seven turnkey Businesses, consists of up to 49 turnkey Practices!

In this case the wheel has as its hub the Client Fulfillment System necessary to produce the great *results* the Enterprise was designed to produce on behalf of its most important customer; and each of the seven spokes—now Businesses–produce the *customers* the hub is intended to serve.

Each of them through what are now 49 Client Acquisition Systems— the spokes of the Business wheel we spoke about earlier.

But now, at this Enterprise level, we add the final piece needed, called the turnkey Leadership System.

An Enterprise

Because managers need leadership if they're ever to provide the essential ingredients needed for the large and growing network of technicians fulfilling their responsibilities for producing the results this great growing enterprise is being designed to produce.

Leadership is the critical function which:

- shows the complete picture of the Enterprise once done, visually, emotionally, functionally, and financially;

- shows the culture that lives within that Enterprise, the spirit of it, the behavior of it, the standards of it, the raison d'être;

- shows the brand of that Enterprise, why it is positioned the way it is positioned, the place it owns in the market it serves; and

- shows the track each individual can pursue, from apprenticeship, to craftsmanship, to mastery—from white belt to black belt— from the very outset to maturity, in the language intended to scale, consistent with the mantra, "every small business a school."

This school, this Enterprise, this cultural phenomenon, this community of aspiring individuals, each of whom is presented with the unparalleled opportunity to excel, all of this is what leadership is about.

All of this is the means and the ends of the process we're engaged in, as we prepare this Enterprise, the cultural phenomenon of it, a system which excels at what it does, which is a match made in heaven for the one who is going to acquire it, because it has accomplished in the real world of "things" what only a small, almost imperceptible number of companies has done.

Thus the reason we call it a "Great Growing Company."

And the reason we did the work that we did.

And the reason for this book, *Beyond The E-Myth—The Evolution of an Enterprise: From a Company of One to a Company of 1,000!*

Let's get started!

PART I

Part I: Chapter One

THE DREAM

I would have you consider that the highest purpose of the human species is to justify the gift of life.

—Norman Cousins, *The Celebration of Life*

No worthwhile venture can be started without a clear and compelling Dream.

Yes, it's an edict promoted throughout entrepreneurdom, the social economy, as well as the academic world. But it is rarely understood in the way we're going to be discussing it here.

A true entrepreneur's Dream is not personal. It's impersonal. It's not about the Dreamer; it's about the consumer.

The Dream we're talking about is the great result you intend to produce in the world through the development of a company which excels at fulfilling that Dream.

And, as we begin this exercise of ours to design, build, launch, and grow your company to scale, it's critical for you to think of your "consumer" in two ways, and in this order:

First will be the consumer who's going to buy your company.

And second will be the consumer who's going to buy your product.

Wait! What? Why in that order?

Because unless, at the outset of this process, you have a clear picture of who's going to buy your company, you will more than likely spend years going after the wrong retail consumer, with the wrong product, and end up creating the wrong company.

Don't want to do that, do we?

For after all, that's what most EVERYONE has done, isn't it?

Spent years—if they've managed to survive at all—working in the wrong company, building the wrong business, all because they started by accepting (or selecting) the wrong customer.

As the old expression goes, working their fingers to the bone, or, more bluntly, working their asses off, nonstop, hoping against hope that in time it will become easier.

And produce more.

But, of course, it doesn't.

And it won't.

You just get older.

Pisser.

A Blank Piece of Paper and Beginner's Mind

To discover your Dream, a dream worthy of the overwhelming amount of energy and capital you're going to have to invest in it, isn't easy.

Above all, it doesn't start out the way you might think—with a sudden realization that THIS is what you were meant to do. That THIS is your calling. There's no bright flash and fade-to-white like in the movies.

No, the Dream we're talking about here starts out with nothing, rather than with something.

It's the *absence* of something which stimulates this kind of dreaming, rather than the *presence* of something.

Indeed, the true Dream is most often completely counterintuitive.

The Dream we're talking about is more likely to arise from the discovery of extreme pain out there, rather than the promise of extreme pleasure in here.

A Great Growing Company is as likely to be catalyzed by watching a guy run his car into a tree as it would be by envisioning a more elegant interior for that very same car.

More by, "What in the hell happened there?" than by, "I love to design car seats."

The Dream of a Great Growing Company is more apt to be inspired by the mind and imagination of an earnestly captivated reporter looking for a great and compelling story, than it would be by a guy who fashions himself becoming the next Henry Ford.

In short, Dreaming, as we're speaking of it here has nothing to do with being inspired to become a great entrepreneur, or to get rich, or to own a large Cabin Cruiser, entertaining and being entertained by 10 nubile, bikini-clad women on it . . . or men!

Dreaming, as we're describing it here, has nothing to do with the millionaire next door, or the billionaire flying his own personal jet, or owning your own island and traveling to exotic places. It is without all of the stuff the famous do (or we're told they do), with fast cars, beautiful friends, and exotic nightlife—hanging with the 1/10th of 1%.

No, while all those trappings might be lovely, entertaining window dressing, they wouldn't fuel what we're about to pursue here.

Instead, they will most certainly distract us from it.

"A blank piece of paper and beginner's mind" means that you're open, empty, interested, curious, and love being that way, so that as stuff happens around you—and within you—you're able to see it, take it in, and turn it into what it's come forth to actually tell you.

"A blank piece of paper and beginner's mind" happens right now, not in the future. It's a state of being, a presence, not a pursuit of something.

That's why so many of the best entrepreneurs in the world tell the paper napkin story with such glee.

And why some of the greatest companies on the planet started out just like that—on a paper napkin.

Why a paper napkin?

Because that's what happened to be available when the idea came through.

They didn't walk around with a bunch of paper napkins in their pockets in anticipation of the great event.

(And please don't say I suggested that!)

Rather, something—a thought, a picture, a flash, an idea, an experience, a fresh awareness—came to them (or through them), whether they were ready for it or not.

And they grabbed whatever was available to capture it—on that paper napkin, that matchbook, that recorder on their phone, the back of that overdue parking ticket.

That's the "blank piece of paper" part.

The "beginner's mind" part was that they were accessible to what "came to them." They were literally an open door. A clear channel. Right then and there. In that very moment.

Most of us, unfortunately, are rarely open doors.

Even now, while you're reading this, it's quite possible that your mind is closing down. Distracted by a conflicting thought pulling you away. That happens to all of us, doesn't it?

Associations form. This thought triggers another thought, another experience, a desire, a fear, a memory from the past, a troubling feeling in the present, a doubt about the future. Something you need to do. Something you planned on doing. Something that has become a part of your programming. Something that didn't work out, or did work out.

Your program is the automated self you've unintentionally become.

The You everyone knows you to be.

The most often False Personality constructed unintentionally out of the maelstrom of conflicting components of your day-to-day script. The part you've been playing. The character you've been fashioned out to become. The life which is living you in what we know to be your "day to day."

All of that—those conflicting thoughts and feelings—those spiraling chains of distractions—the assumptions and the reservations—must be put away as we begin this process of Dreaming.

All that entraps us in our "day to day."

If we are to pursue the unknown as an entrepreneur, it is exactly our "day to day" which must be annihilated.

It is that which I mean when I speak about "A blank piece of paper and beginner's mind." It's the annihilation of our "day to day."

And in that annihilation, a door opens.

And then, the only question is, who walks out of it, and who walks in?

FROM OUT OF E-MYTH TO THE DREAMING ROOM

I've told this story many times, but it's essential that we engage in it here, whether you're familiar with it or not. This is how we begin the formal process of Dreaming in what I've come to call The Dreaming Room.

I created The Dreaming Room™ in 2005, as a response to my many years of frustration with my E-Myth clients.

Since my origination of the E-Myth paradigm in 1977, we had worked with over 100,000 small business clients. We called it coaching.

Clients in every kind of company–attorneys, accountants, doctors, graphic designers, machine shop operators, software engineers, gas station owners, Pilates instructors–you name it.

The strategy we pursued was designed to systematically eliminate the host of frustrations our small business clients experienced in the day to day operation of their small companies.

And we did eliminate them.

Not everyone or every time, of course. But, often enough.

But the frustration I experienced was that few of our clients made the shift from being what I called "technicians suffering from an entrepreneurial seizure" to becoming and–behaving like– true entrepreneurs.

In short, my E-Myth days were spent fixing broken businesses, but not successfully enough fixing the broken mindset required to turn those struggling small companies into abundantly successful large companies.

That shift of mindset, from the technician to the entrepreneur, from a tiny company, completely dependent upon the person who owned it, to an abundantly productive company many times that size, called for more than just working on their existing company, putting the pieces together, as we'd call it.

It called for a wholly new approach to the business of business.

It required an entrepreneurial approach.

It screamed out for inspiration. A fresh insight. An innovative perspective about something going on in the world (in our case, the E-Myth world) which needed fixing, and a determination to do something about it.

Something disruptive. Something definitive. Something highly differentiated to awaken the true entrepreneur within. But in order to do that, we needed to define that.

Meaning, we had to deal with the question: What *is* an entrepreneur?

How is an entrepreneur constituted differently than the usual small business owner?

Do you remember earlier, when I suggested that our Dream comes out of the *nothing* rather than the *something?* So it was in identifying our true entrepreneur.

The overriding question I was called to ask and answer was: What is *missing* in this picture?

What were we missing in all our work with small business owners?

What was the source of their (and our) continuous frustrations?

Why was it so damn difficult for our clients to rise above the entrapment of what I came to call "the tyranny of routine"?

In short, in order to awaken the entrepreneur within, we first had to define what an entrepreneur actually is.

Before the Dreaming could begin, we needed to identify who it was that was going to be dreaming it.

Now we were beginning to tease that new something out of nothing, and it coalesced into the Dream which then informed the creation of the process we ultimately called "in The Dreaming Room."

And that led finally to the realization that an entrepreneur isn't just one person, but four—*a complex of four personalities!*

The Entrepreneur as a Complex of Personalities

It became obvious to me that there were actually four personalities inside of every entrepreneur, each with its own role, each with its own contribution to the emergence of an Enterprise.

Take out any one of those four personalities, and a serious gap would be created in the process of inventing and implementing a successfully emerging company.

Those personalities not only define outcomes, but the linear process through which those outcomes are created.

Those personalities are **The Dreamer, The Thinker, The Storyteller, and The Leader.**

The Dreamer has a Dream.

The Thinker has a Vision.

The Storyteller has a Purpose.

The Leader has a Mission.

Dream. Vision. Purpose. Mission.

The essential raw components of an Enterprise. The essential four components missing in almost every small business.

To think about them in another way:

The Dream is The Great Result.

The Vision is the form the company is going to take.

The Purpose is the profound Impact the company is going to have on its customer.

The Mission is that great business operating system which will enable The Dream, The Vision, and The Purpose to be manifested as an operating enterprise.

In my case, with the E-Myth, my Dream was *"to transform the state of small business worldwide."*

My Vision was *"to invent The McDonald's of small business consulting."*

My Purpose was *"to provide every small business owner with the ability to succeed just like a McDonald's franchise does."*

My Mission was *"to invent the turnkey Business Development Operating System essential for every small company to operate as effectively and efficiently as the most successful of companies do. All at a cost any small business owner could readily afford."*

In short, my Great Growing Company intended to eradicate small business failure from the face of the planet.

I reasoned that with The Dreaming Room process in place (my NewCo), everyone will be able to discover their own Great Result, their own Vision of operating integrity, their own profound customer impact unlike anything ever delivered before, their own systems approach to delivering it at a cost that everyone can afford.

But, for all that to occur, first must be The Dream.

And before The Dream, must be The Dreamer.

THE DREAMER: WHO AM I? WHY AM I HERE?

I led my very first live Dreaming Room™ in December 2005.

There were 35 participants.

None of us knew what was about to happen.

All we knew was that we were going to spend 2½ days together to "awaken the new entrepreneur within."

I'd never led a Dreaming Room™ before. Nor, when we started on that Friday evening, had I prepared anything to do it other than my extreme (and I hoped, not misplaced) confidence in my ability to figure it out while doing it, accompanied by an 11"x17" pad of blank paper— "The Dreaming Room Pad™"—and a bunch of variously colored felt tip pens wrapped in a ribbon we provided to each of our guests.

My intention was to share my frustrations with them, working as I had over the previous years with broken small businesses, and to tell them that, unlike anything I had done before, this weekend was not intended to fix their broken business, or solve their existing problems, but to discover how true entrepreneurs might create, "with a blank piece of paper and beginner's mind."

I assured them that the process would reveal itself to us, as I pursued it at the front of the room, and as they joined at the front of the room in the many "hot seats" we would conduct with any of them courageous enough to engage with me, one-on-one.

And so it began—the first of 59 such Dreaming Rooms™ I would lead over the next five years.

What a revelation those Dreaming Rooms™ were!

To me, and to my unwary participants.

Not one of us was prepared for the realizations that showed up.

How those pads of paper filled up, and were torn up, and then filled up again!

How out of the ordinary were those revelations! Whole hosts of strangers came to visit with and within the participants; people they'd never met before. People who came up to share their lonely stories at the front of the room. People who couldn't sleep any longer, couldn't hide any longer, couldn't stifle their imagination any longer, couldn't lay supine any longer, couldn't deal with their unexpressed guilt, rage, or pain any longer.

Entire new worlds were discovered by each and every one of them. The many barriers to opportunity they'd unintentionally erected over the years exposed themselves in all their obstinate colors.

Couples discovered why their relationships weren't working. Partners discovered why they never should have become partners, given each of their unexpressed needs, their unexpressed desires, and their unexpressed, conflicted, and conflicting perceptions of reality.

"Who am I?" became the overriding question.

"Why am I here?" became the prevailing issue.

"What do I really want?" was batted from pillar to post, as we began to realize that, if we were to truly create a stunningly emergent enterprise, we were all asking the wrong questions.

That, until we discovered who we truly were, how we truly went about our day-to-day business, why the way we were accustomed to doing that was invariably going to produce the very same results we had grown accustomed to, estranged from, and nothing other—until that unimaginably difficult shift occurred, it was unlikely anything other than the false and silly dreams we were creating on our blank pieces of paper, all in lovely brilliant color, would ever truly reveal itself to any of us.

And it was such that we discovered that the key to awakening the new entrepreneur within wasn't to evoke more narcissistic subjectivity, as our culture had suggested, but instead, to evoke a rare form of objectivity, enriched with and by a new form of subjectivity, one with which we had little experience.

And we harnessed that evolved form of subjectivity that we saw was informed by a living matrix of emotional intelligence, and intellectual intelligence, and incased in a freely floating pragmatic intelligence imbued by both and encompassing all.

Emotional Intelligence, Intellectual Intelligence, and Pragmatic Intelligence—which was to invite a supreme liberation of sorts from the unmistakably automated evolution we were all struggling to reject, but within which we had each been imprisoned.

You see, each of us in that Dreaming Room had each come to believe in the myth that we had grown our lives intentionally, when the process we engaged in together in those 2½ days demonstrated to us exactly the opposite to be true.

Indeed, despite how successful most of us had become in our time, instead of the free thinkers we thought ourselves to be, we had become automatons instead.

And that our automatic behaviors—habituated as they were—made it almost impossible to engage in a blank piece of paper with a beginner's mind.

Made it truly almost impossible to create anything original at all.

That the seemingly blank piece of paper in the pad before us was already full before we put a pen to it.

And that the beginner's mind we so proudly pursued was a figment of our obviously untutored imagination. We had long ago given up even the possibility of it.

What then?

THE DREAM IS THE PRODUCT OF THE DREAMER

Indeed, the first task in The Dreaming Room became obvious: that before we discovered our Dream, we first, it seemed, had to discover (or uncover, or recover) our Dreamer.

That our Dream was the product of The Dreamer within as were the Vision, Purpose, and Mission that of The Thinker, The Storyteller, and The Leader within.

That we were *born* with The Dreamer within.

That The Dreamer already existed within us, and it was that capability every one of us already possessed. So, in fact, it wasn't our job to discover it, but to allow it to express itself.

To get out of its way.

To allow it to do its job.

Isn't that astonishing? In The Dreaming Room we each discovered, to one degree or another, that our job was to get out of the way of The Dreamer within.

And, as we did so–and only when we did so—could we fulfill the promise we had each, knowingly or unknowingly, come to fulfill.

And as that occurred to us, we also discovered that each and every one of us was possessed of a uniquely personal, albeit objectively pragmatic, Dreamer.

To Steve, it was about spirituality.

To Lyndon, it was about relationship.

To Judy, it was about love.

To Jim, it was about personal responsibility.

We had no idea why that was so. But, during the 2½ days we spent together, it became absolutely clear that it was so.

The Dream for each of us then became a product of all that.

And in turn an objective.

A Great Result.

A possibility which took form in the statement we, each of us, created to express it.

As said, in my case, "to transform the state of small business worldwide."

That was to become the core platform upon which everything I was to create from that point forward was launched.

So, it became clear to me that it was in The Dreaming Room that *Beyond The E-Myth,* this very book, was born.

So Who Is Going to Buy Our Company?

Once it was clear what we intended to do, and why we intended to do it, it became obvious who would be interested in buying us.

Just make a list.

In our case, it would be the company that created QuickBooks, or American Express, or Microsoft, or maybe the Gallup Organization, or one of the dozens of investor groups that specialize in funding or incubating NewCo's from their very beginnings, or, or, or . . .

Why?

It's so obvious isn't it?

If we were to invent the Power Source for Small Business™; develop the systems at the core of it; successfully enroll small business owners to implement it; and then successfully deliver the improved performance each of our clients desired; and then, proof of the pudding, build it to scale; in the hands of ordinary people; all at low cost, not at high cost; to provide every one of our small business clients with an extreme competitive advantage—and to be able to PROVE it . . .

Of course we would be acquired, in a virtual auction of our wares.

That's why thinking of one's company as a product is so important to this process.

Because just like a product, your company has to be packaged.

Visually, emotionally, functionally, and financially.

A turnkey methodology which produces exactly the results it was intended to produce.

In our case, in every small business on the planet.

Just like Microsoft set out to do. Just like Apple. Just like QuickBooks. Just like McDonald's. Just like Google. Just like just about every Great Growing Company you've ever seen or heard about.

And to achieve that objective, you have to see it when it's done. You have to see it out there at the end of the process, exactly as you intend it to look.

Because the seeing of it is essential if you're ever going to show it to someone else.

Which, at that point in time, when the buyer comes to your door, sounds like: "Let me show you what we've done!"

"Let me show you what I dreamed up."

Done.

Now let's take a look at your Vision. ✤

Part I: Chapter Two

THE VISION

The intensity with which you impress your subconscious with a picture of your plan directly affects the speed with which the subconscious will go to work to attract the picture's physical counterpart by inspiring you to take the right steps.

—Napoleon Hill, *Napoleon Hill's Keys to Success*

Now you can see how the Dream creates the foundation for everything that's to follow.

The first step in the process we're calling "The Hierarchy of Growth."

Without a clear and compelling Dream, there is no "there, there." There is no forward-driving force. No source for inspiring the tradition lying at the heart of your company. There is no "meaning" as Viktor Frankl wrote about in "Man's Search for Meaning."

There is no "Great" in your Great Growing Company.

The Dream, then, is where the "Great" lives.

The Dream is what drives your Vision, your Purpose, and your Mission.

In the marketplace of ideas and actions, the Dream is who you are.

The Dream is your being, your philosophy, your existential reality, your purpose, your light in the dark surrounding it.

The Dream is the reason your company is alive.

It's your *zeitgeiste.*

Dr. Martin Luther King proclaimed, "I have a dream!"

And so must you.

But, having tentatively arrived at your Dream, discovering it, becoming convinced of it, now it must be given a form, if it is to be implemented.

Here we turn your quest into action.

Here we're going to turn your Dream into an operating enterprise.

Thus, the Vision.

The Vision tells you what your company is going to look like, act like, and be like, in order to produce the outcome, the Great Result, your Dream has set out before you.

The Vision frames and defines the great HOW through which your Dream is going to be manifested in the world and on the street, rather than just in your imagination.

In other words, your Dream must become "street-smart" if it's to stand a chance of succeeding.

So, in establishing your Vision, you're looking for a street-smart business model to emulate.

That does not mean you're going to become what someone else has created—you're not going to become McDonald's—but you *are* going to emulate this most successful street model by taking it apart and putting it back together again to fit your purpose—to get the results you want.

Remember, all of this work we're doing is about getting results.

We're not creating *only* to be creative.

We're not innovating *simply* to be innovative.

We're not going into business, *just* to go into business.

We've got a serious end in mind.

And, to discover how to get there, we're going to want to study the laws of the universe in which we live to most effectively produce exactly what we're looking for.

And what, again, ARE we looking for in the development of our Vision?

We're looking for a SYSTEM that has already proven itself.

An operating system that has already enabled an entrepreneur to achieve the sort of end result we are setting out to achieve; one that contains a turnkey capability to scale a turnkey company that produces the result we've set out to produce.

What better example can I give you than McDonald's?

McDonald's: The Perpetual Motion Machine of Pure Performance

Yes, at the heart of your Vision, providing the bones for the HOW of your Dream, which provides for the scaling of your company for sale, resides McDonald's.

Because—and this is important—at the heart of McDonald's beats the word **"turnkey."**

Understand, "turnkey" is not simply a mindset exclusive for McDonald's; it's a systemic reality at the core of every great object and phenomena on the planet.

Where turnkey doesn't exist, random rules.

Where systems thinking isn't alive and well, chaos is.

Adventures in Turnkey:

I flew from San Diego to Houston on a 737. It left on time, gained altitude, headed east according to a pre-determined route and a rigid system of ground control, pilot training and feedback, and self-correcting instrumentation, and it landed on time and systematically ushered out its passengers. Turnkey.

I drove my car from San Marcos to Carlsbad, following operational routines that were instilled in me 60-plus years ago, on interconnecting surface streets and highways that are laid out to intersect with my starting point and destination. Turnkey.

I'm writing this chapter with MS Word. Of course, I have (what at first may seem to be) an unlimited, infinite number of choices I can make in selecting words, concepts, and length of paragraphs—I have, after all, a virtual blank sheet—but the process of booting my laptop, opening MS Word, ordering up a blank template (or a saved document), and transferring these thoughts to that electronic page is routine, fixed, and predictable. In fact, in the final analysis, so are my creative choices, because I've chosen to conform to the standards and conventions of all of my previous books. The content, of course, is new but the style itself has become a disciplined part of the system. Turnkey.

So now, I'm inventing (or looking for an existing model that could be re-purposed to support) a new platform for operating a small company. And I know that if it isn't turnkey, it will be a disaster.

My Vision, then, is that of a turnkey Enterprise; built to operate in exactly the way I intend it to; producing exactly the result I intend it to; and providing to our customers exactly the outcome I intend it to. Just like Lockheed Martin does every day in its Skunk Works. Just like Supercuts does every hour, or Starbucks does every minute.

And, in order for me to be able to accomplish that, (or, indeed, any of the founding entrepreneurs in the above enterprises), I need to either emulate a standard operating reality which someone has already created, or begin at the very beginning and invent my own from scratch.

The problem with "from scratch" is that it's ignoring everything that has probably already been learned about the process.

Which doesn't, by the way, fly in the face of "a blank piece of paper and beginner's mind;" it simply augments it.

You see, as we begin, as we pursue the outcome we're intending to produce, as we're inventing a new machine to achieve a result not yet achieved by the old machines out here doing what they're doing, what I hope to find is a way that's already been used to produce a different outcome than the one I'm intending to produce, but operating with exactly the same standards and expectations, while dealing with the very same kinds of constraints, frustrations, conditions, circumstances, and reality I know we're going to face in the creation, operation, and management of our outcome.

Thus McDonald's has become, for me—and coincidentally, for you—a perfect premise upon which you and I get to benefit from what they've already accomplished, making McDonald's what I've come to call "the most successful small business in the world."

So, in my case, as the author of *The E-Myth,* my Vision was "to invent the McDonald's of small business consulting."

The picture I had in mind was a consulting system organized and orchestrated to such a standardized degree that I could then teach a relative novice—the McDonald's kid—to deliver it.

It was an outrageous idea.

All such ideas are outrageous.

If it weren't outrageous somebody would have already done it.

But to my way of thinking it was all so obvious.

I asked, how come nobody has done this before?

To my way of thinking, it was ridiculously simple, that when we solved this problem—the operating failure of almost every small business— the economic performance of the world would be transformed.

Since the economic performance of the world resided in the hands of small business, not in the hands of the largest companies on the planet, what a miracle it would be once we figured this out.

And to me, figuring this out seemed like a walk in the park.

Why couldn't we?

It was just nuts and bolts and the like, wasn't it?

And so we did.

Our Dream gave it energy.

Our Vision gave it form.

Our actions gave it the life needed to produce it in reality.

Your Vision Becomes Your Franchise Prototype

Now this is a very interesting and important point, and it has everything to do with the underlining premise of this book, where I say "from a company of one to a company of 1,000!"

It is here that you must understand that I'm not suggesting that you must create an enterprise with 1,000 employees in order to achieve your Great Result.

Instead, I'm *emphatically* saying that you must create a company that has the *ability to achieve that objective* and, in order to demonstrate that ability, you must build out the platform to prove it.

The platform to prove it is what I call your Franchise Prototype.

Your Franchise Prototype will be one small business, primed, ready and able to grow a very big one. I call that one small business your **Practice.**

You'll remember that your Practice is the three-legged stool, combining Lead Generation, Lead Conversion and Client Fulfillment—the three essential systems—into a turnkey capability prepared to scale.

What I'm suggesting is, that no matter what you intend the Great Result of your Enterprise to be, to realize it, to fashion it in such a way to definitely be able to realize it, you must design, build, launch, and grow that Practice just like McDonald's did.

From its very beginning—here in the Dreaming and Visioning stage—you intentionally and consciously and audaciously design, build, launch, and grow your company as if you intend to franchise it.

And once you get what I just said, you should very quickly understand why I've persistently and consistently used the model called McDonald's as the perfect exemplar for every entrepreneur, creating any enterprise, producing any outcome it intends to produce.

That foundational Dream, married to the systemic McDonald's model, framing the Vision, makes it sustainable and expandable.

The system itself made manifest in the Vision provides for scalability, innovation, and expansion, while keeping the core objective intact and supreme.

Your Dream gives it energy.

Your Vision gives it form.

Your actions give it the life needed to produce it in reality. ❧

THE PURPOSE

I can't myself raise the winds that might blow us, or this ship, into a better world. But I can at least put up the sail so that, when the wind comes, I can catch it.

—E.F. Schumacher, *Good Work*

So now we have a Dream (the WHAT) and a Vision (the HOW) of the company we're about to create to exceed all expectations. We're not perfectly clear, but we're getting there. The Dreamer has a Dream, The Thinker has a Vision.

Now we're ready to assume the role of <u>The Storyteller</u>, to decide WHO specifically we're about to create extreme value for, and what form that extreme value takes in the lives of these most important customers. And we're going to need to explain it to them in a way that captures their attention and inspires (or enflames) them with the power of the idea.

Our Purpose.

Over the years at my speaking events I've told my audiences that there are three kinds of people in every audience I've spoken to. People who hate me, people who love me, and people who don't know what just happened.

Truth is, it's hard to take the people who hate me. They're always so vocal. They're reading this book right now and spoiling for trouble. They say I don't say enough. They say I say more than I need to. They say that I'm self-aggrandizing, arrogant, a terrible writer, stupid about what's really true about business, airy fairy, self-indulgent, it goes on and on.

It's truly astonishing to me to read the reviews of my books.

One reviewer says: "DO NOT READ THIS BOOK!"

A second says: "AMAZING!"

A third compares me to the great corporate guru, Peter Drucker!

A fourth compares me to the Devil!

All, **reviewing the same book!**

"A complete waste of time!" "The most important book I've ever read!"

That's what happens when you set out to tell a Story. You bump up against the perceptions (and, therefore, the reality) of each person listening.

And I hope that's what will happen to you.

Because when it does—and it will, if you persist—you'll know you've struck pay dirt!

But keep in mind, not everyone is going to be your most important customer. But when you set out and set down your Story, you're going to assume that they are. Because, at the onset, you just don't know whether that person in your audience who hates you might hear something that opens his mind to an alternative reality—that challenges his perception—and breaks through his armor and stimulates his imagination and compels him to accept the challenge of "what if?"

And you don't know if that person who loves you, (who, it would seem, at first, is your ideal customer), may truly love the *idea* of what you're proposing, but will never, ever make the commitment, take the critical first step or leap of faith to actually become your best customer.

And, finally, you don't know and can't say with certainty that the person who comes in and leaves seemingly perplexed and (okay) clueless, won't one day soon (or years later) experience an epiphany (or, perhaps what I used to call an "entrepreneurial seizure"), and something you said or showed him that he didn't really see at the time is now the picture he can't get out of his head!

You Actually Have Two Important Customers

I want to remind you here that you really have two most important customers:

- The first customer, of course, is your strategic customer; the one who's going to buy your company when you're done.

- The second is the one we're creating this Story for: the retail customer for your product or service. This is the primary and direct recipient of your Great Result.

In my case, my *retail* customer has always been those millions of small business owners, or those who think they have an idea for a world-changing business—who are committed and ready to break the mold. So it follows that my strategic customer would be a company that shares my customer base—that small business owner who is struggling to succeed—to move forward in growth–but is tragically trapped, working his tail off in the day-to-day tyranny of routine. So, the buyer of my company would be someone like Intuit. Or Google. Or Apple. Or UPS. Or Microsoft. Or Salesforce. Or Citibank. Or American Express. Or the U.S. Chamber of Commerce. Or the Small Business Administration–any large company or agency that can appreciate the exponential value they could bring to our mutual most important customers by incorporating my company within their service offerings. My strategic customer has as their most important customer my most important customer—business owners or business dreamers with perceived or even unperceived needs, which need to be filled! These companies are in the business of identifying some of those needs, and providing intelligent technology, tools, information, or financial support to satisfy them, in some cases, long before their customers even perceive they need them.

There are tools and devices we're buying today that do things we never needed to do, and are consuming and changing the behavior of all people in ways no one could have predicted, or even believed possible. But in all of the above cases, it's not just about the software, or the tools, or the support, but the *mindset.* These companies, and countless more just like them, in their own unique fashion, are changing the ways their customers think about their lives and how to live them. They're in the business of changing minds, which has a direct link to their behavior.

Would it not be a discrete and profound advantage for a company like that to possess the ability to "transform the state of small business worldwide"?

To fundamentally transform the way its customers think about business? About the metrics of management, of leadership, of organizational development, of strategy, of positioning, of extreme differentiation? Or, even more remarkably, the need to learn how to manage, to lead, to market, to organize, given that there are tools being designed to completely eliminate the need for you to do that?

Shouldn't every company be determined to nurture its customers to grow simply because it cares? And because it well knows that as its customers grow, it grows as well?

As you begin to actually take that in, and begin to discover your true Dream, and see the significance of that ability to truly *produce* the stunning result you've expressed in your Dream, then and only then can you fully understand why your "company of one" would be heroic in both the eyes of your retail customer as well as in the eyes of your strategic customer for its ability to do that.

So now, let's pursue your Purpose.

The Storyteller Needs a Great Story

The Dreamer and The Thinker require someone to go out into the world to tell the Great Story they've given birth to.

Well, that would be *you!*

You're that person.

You're The Dreamer, The Thinker, and now The Storyteller whose responsibility it is to define, describe, create, and convince your most important customer that their world is about to be transformed, to become significantly better. That it's *important* for that to happen.

One of the greatest Dreamers, Thinkers, and Storytellers of all time, the Reverend Dr. Martin Luther King Jr., told the Story of his Dream in the turbulent waning half of the 20th Century:

See the video—**www.beyondemyth.com/MLK-Video**

Read the script—**www.beyondemyth.com/MLK-VideoScript**

If you took the time to listen to Dr. King, or read his script, congratulations.

If you didn't, I'd strongly suggest that you do so now, and that you listen to it or read it all the way to the end.

Because, by listening to King's expression of his Dream, you begin to get a taste of what true passion is all about. And why, until your story evokes true passion—and is created *by* true passion—you will never understand why so few "companies of one" grow beyond the very ordinary. It's a place for the owner to work—but that's all.

Additionally, other than to call for something great to happen, the Dream does something else:

By just *beginning* the process of Dreaming, the founder of "a Company Of One" is transported to a completely new place in his or her mind.

Remarkably, just the *prospect* of Dreaming—the *willingness* to do it—takes you to a completely different place in your mind.

The place which stimulates your imagination.

The place which inspires you to go higher than you've ever imagined going before.

Most of my readers came along with me early on when I articulated the simple, clear-cut premise that "the system is the solution" and that the model for a successful Franchise Prototype was one in which "systems run the business and people run the system."

But too many stopped there.

They said: "I got it."

And I said: "No, you haven't."

Because, over time—and I've been immersed in this arena for over 40 years—I've generated and witnessed all sorts of reactions from small business people of every kind.

From the most agnostic to the most argumentative, to the most hostile, to the most inspired.

And I've asked far, far more from them than just a set of systems; I've been bargaining for a significantly higher state of mind from a leader if his or her company is to be put on a path of true greatness.

And I continue to proselytize this message of the higher mindset, with what some might see as fanatical fervor, but I'm a witness. I've been a party to what happens when small business owners wake up, become inspired, begin to believe they can actually create something <u>significantly more important than anything they've ever created before</u>, *and,* I've done it myself.

So it is that it's here, in these trenches, so to speak, at this stage of our conversation, that you begin to understand this absolutely essential exercise you've got to go through to discover your Story, to exercise your most imaginative, innovative muscles to inspire and motivate the people for whom it's most important.

The people you intend to tell it to.

Note, I said, "tell it to," not "sell it to."

The Story is not an "elevator pitch."

When done the right way, it goes much, much deeper than that.

True, the aim of an "elevator pitch" is to capture your listener's attention, but capturing their attention is only the beginning of the challenge. Because today it is significantly and increasingly more difficult to get their attention, let alone sustain it. Today, there are digital Storytellers galore out there, with more information for your customer than ever before, more webinars, teleconferences, seminars, free stuff with every pop-up than ever before. In our increasingly noisy marketplace, it is increasingly more difficult for you to capture and secure their attention. So today, more than ever before, you need to learn HOW to do it well—*you can't just wing it anymore.*

And know, too, that the more determined you are to capture your audience's attention, the more criticism you're bound to create.

Getting Down to The Heart of The Matter

The Story your Storyteller is about to tell must get down to the heart of the matter.

It must strike to the core of your audience's frustrations.

Core frustrations. Not *all* frustrations.

Meaning, your Story has got to address one thing, and only one thing.

One thing that stands out as the greatest obstacle in the way of your audience's ability to achieve an objective that is most important to them.

The question is, how do you find out what that "one thing" is?

Simple. You talk to them.

Or, you get someone else to talk to them.

(We'll provide you with a system to accomplish that later on in Chapter Six).

To provide you with a compelling example of your Great Story, I'm going to provide you with a link to three of the greatest stories in Chapter Twelve.

And, in the meantime, here is a link to a short video from a "live" Dreaming Room, in which I lead a hot-seat participant through this very conversation, and where I fulfill the role of the Storyteller)— **www.beyondemyth/DR-HotSeat.**

And now, let's go on to the fourth essential step toward awakening the entrepreneur within you, and within the founding of your new company, with the Leader and the Mission. ♣

THE MISSION

They see the pattern, understand the order, experience the vision.
—Peter Drucker, *The New Society*

We've now identified, at least temporarily, your Dream, Vision, and Purpose. The building blocks for the foundation for your new company.

I say, temporarily, because as we move forward you'll begin to discover what's missing in this picture.

You'll begin to become sensitive to the finer shades of it. The stuff you hadn't considered. The "color commentary" behind your true motivation, about what's truly moving you to pursue this process.

You'll begin to discover how strategic thinking can appear to be abstract.

Indeed, how abstract the idea of your *life* can be.

How humbling and difficult it is to take yourself seriously.

To take your *life* seriously.

To take seriously the fact that your life is going to end.

And, so, to take the future seriously.

To take your exit strategy seriously.

What kind of strength and determination and stamina will it take to overcome your fear that this will simply become a mirror of your past? That it won't work out? That it is too full of surprises?

You have no control over what those surprises might be. (Or they wouldn't be a surprise!)

Why do you suppose that people don't plan?

Why do you suppose that people don't save money?

Why do you suppose that over 50% of marriages end in divorce?

Why is it that most small businesses fail with alarming regularity?

Why is it that 70% of average college graduates enter their first year out of school encumbered with $35,000 in debt?[1]

Why is it, do you suppose, that our federal debt is now at $20 trillion and rising by $3 billion a day?

[1] http://www.marketwatch.com/story/class-of-2015-has-the-most-student-debt-in-us-history-2015-05-0

Why is it, do you suppose, that more often than not my readers tell me that my book is *the only book they've read* since graduating from high school?

Why is it, do you suppose, that we're so hopelessly enslaved by Twitter, Facebook, Instagram, TV streaming services, 24-hour TV news, and broadcast entertainment access that in 2015, we spent an average of more than *10 hours per day consuming media?*

We carry our smart phones with us wherever we go. We wake up with them, go to sleep with them, feel lost if we've somehow misplaced them.

Why is it, do you suppose, that as our technology becomes smarter and smarter, we become less and less so?

I'd submit that it's because of these conditions—highlighted by the random facts above that simply illustrate today's not so subtle reality of being human—that the process we're engaged in here is so damned difficult to sustain. To see it through. To not lose our place. To make it real. To take it seriously.

How can we take our Dream seriously, if we don't take ourselves seriously?

How can we imagine our Vision as a true Vision to be cherished and advanced—rather than a bit of homework we've done—if we are unable to anchor our sights in what's real?

If we don't take ourselves seriously, how can we take our Vision seriously?

How can we possibly presume to imagine that we will discover the means to transform the state of our potential customers, when we can't even transform our own state, can't even imagine what it would take to do so, and can't take ourselves seriously enough even to carve out the space to engage in the endeavor?

How is it that Steve Jobs was able to create Apple, when we haven't even created a job worth pursuing?

How is it that Google was invented?

What was the impetus and catalyst for those two friends who launched Pinterest?

How is it that we find ourselves so lacking?

Where does that creative, entrepreneurial energy come from?

Which brings us to the Leader.

The Leader and The Mission

The Dreamer, The Thinker, The Storyteller, and finally, The Leader.

Without the Leader, none of what we've done stands a chance of becoming a reality.

It's the Leader who makes things happen.

It's the Leader, who takes the Dream, Vision, and Purpose most seriously. So much so that he or she devotes her or his life to declaring them out loud, to realizing them, to manifesting them, and to making them come true.

The Leader infuses the Dream, Vision, and Purpose with the energy needed to turn them from thoughts and ideas and notions into substance. The Leader infuses the heartfelt, but still premature, Dream with passion and soul, and gives it a life of its own, outside of the incubator—taking it beyond the idea.

The Leader is on a Mission to turn the Dream, the Vision, and the Purpose into commitments, promises, and actions, charged with the earnest intent to touch the hearts of the people who are going to be needed to do the real work—and to believe you, not just *in* you. Those who will keep your promise. To take your promise seriously. And join you in the Mission.

The Leader has a Mission.

You're the Leader.

Your Mission is to turn your Dream, Vision, and Purpose into an Enterprise that fulfills your Dream's Great Result, your Vision's Great Growing Company, and your Purpose's promise in the real world.

Your Mission as the Leader is to direct, instruct, and inspire the designing, building, launching, and growing of the systems which will make all of that possible.

Now it is time to get intimately familiar with what is destined to become your turnkey Client Fulfillment System, your turnkey Client Acquisition System, your turnkey Management System, and yes, your turnkey Leadership System.

So, let's get started! ❧

PART II

Part II: Chapter Five

ON THE STREET

New ways of thinking about familiar things can release new energies and make all manner of things possible.

—Charles B. Handy, *The Age of Unreason*

NewCo starts out on the street.

With calls on your prospective customers.

You've already determined who that is going to be. You've already decided in the most general sense what you believe you're going to provide them—your product—but you haven't yet begun to have that conversation to the degree you must, and that's where this chapter begins. On the Street. Meeting face-to-face with your Central Demographic Model Consumer. Asking them the most important questions you can ask. Everything begins on the street—in the marketplace—because the marketplace reflects the heart, mind, and experience which is the life of your customer.

So, being on the street doesn't lead with a promise, as a sales call does. It starts with questions.

And those questions suggest, with all sincerity, a determined interest to discover what's true about the heart, mind and experience of your prospective customer.

And those questions begin on the street, where your customer lives.

The Most Important Questions:

Years ago, when I started my very first company, way back when in 1977, there were just the two of us. It was called The Michael Thomas Corporation. I was Michael. He was Thomas. The company was what we thought we would do, to become the very first coaching company of its kind. Coaching small business owners about how to create a successful company out of the typically disorganized company they owned and operated.

Our straight commissioned sales people walked down every street where a business lived, walked in every single door and asked for the owner. And of course we asked it face-to-face. And when the owner wasn't there (or was hiding!) we'd ask whoever we met there, "Who is the owner? What's his or her name? How long has the business been here? And who are you?" (the person we're speaking to), and, "How long have you worked here? And do you like it? And what do you do?" And on and on and on until the owner would come out and ask us who WE were! And then the conversation continued, or not—many times not—but that was only the first call of many calls we were determined to make on every single small company in the city we inhabited.

And in each and every call we got to know the owner better, the business better, and the people in the business better.

And all of that led up to "the invitation."

The invitation was to attend a free seminar (we called it a "meeting" then) called, "Key Frustrations in a Small and Growing Business and What to Do About It!"

If you've ready any of my other books, you probably already know about what I just told you, but it is important that I share it with you now; because what led up to the seminar, and what led up to what followed the seminar, was all about telling our prospective client that not only did we know him or her, better than they knew themselves, but that we knew something nobody else in our field— business consulting—knew.

In short, because we knew our prospective client better than anyone else on the planet did—and we would prove that to them in the seminar—we could provide our clients with something nobody else could provide them.

And what we could and would provide them was, in one word, freedom.

Freedom from the "key frustrations" our seminar was going to address in a way and in a form that those frustrations had never been addressed before.

Think about that. From a cold call to a hot call. Door to door. Live people calling on live people. Not a machine. Not a database. But the most rudimentary, archaic process imaginable. And we could do it, because we knew something about OUR business nobody else knew. And we knew something about (their) small business nobody else on the planet knew.

Why? Because we asked them. We asked them the most important question anybody could ever ask them (and rarely bothers):

"Who Are You?"

A lot has happened since those days. In many ways, just about everything has happened since those early days, where Tom was the inside guy, and I was the outside guy. The internet happened. Apple happened. Microsoft happened. Google happened. SurveyMonkey happened. Salesforce happened. Oh my goodness, when you think about it, everything has happened since those relatively innocent days.

But, while it's true that everything has happened to change the face of business both large and small, something quite stunning hasn't happened since 1977.

And that is people.

People aren't any different today than they were then.

And by that I don't mean the habits of people.

The habits of people have changed dramatically.

People didn't walk around with their smart phones in 1977.

People didn't do Facebook or LinkedIn in 1977.

In 1977, people weren't distracted by the gazillion bits of information and apps they're distracted by today, and will become increasingly more so in the years ahead.

Still, today, we, as human beings, are no smarter than we were in 1977. And, if anything, dumber by far.

The machine does much of what we used to do.

The machine thinks for us.

The machine has become, instead of a tool, the replacement of our minds.

Use it (our minds) or lose it has become a reality today.

And, since we are less inclined to use it, we are most definitely losing it.

Our power to think is being rapidly deteriorated.

It may have started with a murmur at the introduction of the electronic calculator. Those remarkable hand-held, battery-operated marvels that came out of places like Friden and Texas Instruments in the early '80s that could perform geometric, algebraic, trigonomic and logarithmic functions that used to require (as some of my readers will recall) the memorization of tables, formulas, rules, and charts. These calculators were the original "plug and play"; and, as their prices dropped and their availability increased, they became ubiquitous in our world. Finally, our schools began to permit, and, ultimately, require them for math classes!

And, while it made all mathematical problem solving seemingly quicker and easier, it also accelerated our inability to do even the most simple addition, subtraction, division, or multiplication in our heads.

Today, "it" thinks.

We don't.

Which is also the reason why this process we're engaged in is so damned difficult, so hard.

You have to use your mind to do it. You can't delegate it to your computer.

And because, today, with the astonishing reach we have to multi-billions of us instantaneously and worldwide, we have come to believe that we're significantly more connected today, with significantly more potential customers.

When, in reality, we're not truly connected at all.

"It" is.

And "It" ain't you.

Or, believe it or not, "It" ain't them, either.

And the problem is, we don't know that.

We've actually come to believe that the people in our "database" are "friends."

That our digital outreach, and our cleverness, and our Google-invested intelligence, means we actually know the "database" we're connected with.

When, in fact, we don't.

True, we might know the specifics—the data—better than ever before.

What our "database" does on a Friday night. Why they do it. How many different ways they do it. What kind of car they drive when they leave their home to do it. And what kind of home they've left, and who they left with?

But, data replaces relationship. Relationship becomes data. People become markets.

Markets become people.

And the world as we knew it becomes zeros and ones.

And those zeros and ones can never adequately ask or answer the most important question that we asked way back then in 1977, and that you need to ask today:

"Who are you?"

Certainly today, with a flick of the technologically induced wrist, I can reach 100,000 prospects, all at once. Through a book, an email, a blog, a podcast—in all cases, whether archaic and rudimentary or sophisticated and contemporary, there exists a communication channel and device, all pre-programmed to touch the imagination and interest of—in my case—small business owners. Or, in your case, whomever it is you're determined to attract to YOUR seminar, webinar, teleconference, or store.

So, it CAN be achieved.

And the point is, you've got to know them.

Know them better than they know themselves.

So that you can do something for them.

Something they can't do for themselves.

But, being able to reach them isn't the same as <u>knowing</u> them.

Let's take a closer look at how that all works. ❧

THE PROCESS

You must do the thing you think you cannot do.

—Eleanor Roosevelt

I want to apologize to you. What you just read in Chapter Five, ON THE STREET, must have seemed like a sales process.

Meaning, send out the troops to make cold calls on small businesses, invite them to a seminar, and sell them your service.

If you've been at all active in today's business world, you've already seen that, heard that, been told that. That's Info-Marketing 101, yes?

But that's not what we did, nor for the reason you might think.

We did it to truly find out who our customer was.

We did it to truly find out what was going on in the mind of our small business owner.

We did it to test our assumptions, and to discover his.

We did it because we truly had no idea whether our assumptions were correct or completely off the mark.

And, if our assumptions about our prospective client and our conclusions about our business model were incorrect, then what would we do?

And, if they were correct, how did they actually show up in the day-to-day reality of a small business, in ways other than what we assumed?

This was our period of due diligence; we were researching the strength of our assumptions and preparing to design our system solutions.

So, you should know, too, that we didn't send anybody out on the street until *I* had first gone out on the street to develop and then perfect our system for doing so. To perfect our research system.

In other words, at the very outset of The Michael Thomas Corporation, I was the guinea pig.

I was the first to test our system.

I was the first to fail at it.

And I was the very first to succeed at it.

I was working IN The Job, up to my neck, while also working ON The Job—to perfect and codify it.

Just as you need to do.

Making calls. Making calls. Making calls.

Not to *sell* anything, but to develop the know-how, and the way most efficiently and consistently to find the truth that would guide us to discover exactly what it would take to fulfill our Dream "to transform the state of small business worldwide."

That was critical to our becoming the leader of the pack. Because we knew that once we figured this thing out, lots would follow in our footsteps. And they certainly did. The business of business coaching is now a *multi-billion-dollar* marketplace!

But that all started when Tom and I inaugurated our research to confirm the truth behind our dream–with me walking down the streets, in 1977, knocking on the doors of all those small companies in San Mateo, California.

Asking questions.

THE PROCESS BEGAN WITH THE QUESTIONS

The first question we asked was this: *"Hi. Can I ask you a few questions?"*

And the answer was always: *"Who are you?"*

And our answer was always: *"I'm Michael, with The Michael Thomas Corporation, and we're engaged in a research project, talking to small business owners to find out what makes small businesses tick here in*

San Mateo. Just a few questions. Where would it be best to do it?" (With a smile.)

And that was it.

And the research questions?

- *"If you could think of the most difficult problem a small business owner has, what would that be for you?"*

And after they answered–and they always answered–our second question would be . . .

- *"What difficulties does that create for you? How does that show up in your business?"*

And after they answered—and they always answered—our third question would . . .

- *"If you could make a list, what has worked best to solve that problem for you?"*

And after they answered question number three—and they always answered—the next thing we'd do was say:

"Well, I want to thank you, Mr. Jones, for taking the time to answer my questions. It's going to be very helpful to us as we learn more about small businesses in San Mateo and how to help them. As a thank-you for your help, I'd like to give you a gift from my company—a free seat in **"A Meeting with Owners"** *of small businesses here in San Mateo. It's officially*

called: ***"Key Frustrations in a Small and Growing Business and What to Do About It!"*** *(handing him the brochure). "We're holding it next Thursday at 9 o'clock in the morning, or the same day at 7 o'clock in the evening. It's three hours long, and it's the product of what we've learned talking to owners like you. There are usually 30 to 40 business owners there. Which time would be better for you, Mr. Jones, next Thursday at 9 am or at 7 pm?"*

And then we'd register them for the seminar.

But, that was only the beginning of our research, of course.

The very next step was setting the stage for the really serious questions.

SETTING THE STAGE FOR A RELATIONSHIP

A critical part of your Client Fulfillment System—what and how you deliver what it is you promise and your customer seeks—is establishing your point of view.

Your point of view is the position you're taking in that world you've identified as your own.

That point of view can only be established genuinely after you've demonstrated the truth of it in the heart, mind, and experience of your customer.

Let me say that another way: You are only going to get the attention of, and impact the heart, mind, and experience of, your customer, *after* you've confirmed <u>who</u> your customer is, <u>why</u> they behave the way they do, <u>what</u> their frustrations are, what they <u>do</u> about them, and, finally, what is the overriding cause for those frustrations.

In short, the truth that we uncovered and confirmed in all of our initial, street-level questioning was that the *frustrations are only symptoms of an underlying problem.*

Your point of view is being created to eliminate that underlying problem.

That underlying problem is always a strategic problem, not a tactical problem.

Meaning, that underlying strategic problem is the cause of your customer's chronic dysfunction—so frequently manifested by their greatest frustrations.

So few small business owners understood what their underlying problem was. Mostly, they thought their problems were the frustrations themselves.

Not enough money.

Can't find good enough people.

Can't get enough customers.

All frustrations, of course, but none of them the underlying problem. So what was it that we came to understand to be the underlying problem? ❧

Part II: Chapter Seven

THE UNDERLYING PROBLEM

The place to improve the world is first in one's own heart and head and hands, and then work outward from there.

—Robert Persig, *Zen and the Art of Motorcycle Maintenance*

LOOKING FOR THE TRUTH

We truly set out at the very beginning of our company to become "the preeminent provider of small business development services worldwide."

And to do that, we had to discover the underlying problem that was the root cause for the absolute chaos that existed at the heart of the small business economy.

We had to discover why most small businesses failed, and what to do about it.

This was not a marketing solution; this was our operating reality.

We were looking for the truth.

Because, until and unless we discovered the truth underlying the extreme failure—the endemic problem—residing at the heart of the small business economy, we would not, could not, stand a chance of becoming the leader in our chosen field, the field of small business consulting.

And we were determined to become the leader in the field by creating an operating reality unlike anything that had ever been created before.

THE SEARCH

We were on the hunt for what was missing in the picture of every small business whose doors we'd walked through. We were on a search.

And the search constituted all the questions we needed to ask, and the answers those questions elicited.

Not only the answers to the questions we asked when we first met these business owners, but were about to ask of every invited seminar attendee, and the questions every invited seminar attendee needed to ask of him or herself.

In other words, it wasn't just that we were on a search, it was that our success depended upon our small business owners—our seminar attendees—becoming inspired to go on a search of their own.

Without them being inspired to do that, the process would come to naught.

So, it was our intention in the Key Frustrations Seminar to provoke our attendees to see the truth in a way they had never seen it before.

We wanted to put into question the very way they went to business every day.

We intended that the very idea of what a small business is would be challenged, and in a very dramatic way.

We needed our attendees to see that there were small businesses in this world which operated in a fashion completely foreign to what our small business owners did, or even thought to do, every day.

And those companies did what they did because the idea of what they set out to do was so dramatically different from what our small business owners set out to do.

Those other small businesses weren't in fact small businesses at all.

They were small businesses, but they were small businesses that had set out to become very big businesses.

They were small businesses focused on equity, not on income.

They were small businesses organized to grow exponentially, and in the only way growth can happen exponentially, by building the system for growth at the very heart of their business.

Those small businesses were started to grow.

Our small businesses weren't.

And if they were, they were going to fail at it.

Our job was to make certain they didn't.

REVEALING THE UNDERLYING PROBLEM

And so it was, that as we opened our free Key Frustration Seminar, and welcomed our invited attendees, each a small business owner—an owner-operator—we told them that, with all due respect, everything they thought they knew was wrong!

We told them, boldly, that the big underlying problem that was the source of all of the frustrations they'd shared with us was that the owner-operator of the small business was not an entrepreneur, but a "technician suffering from an entrepreneurial seizure."

Nobody had ever told them that before.

Nobody had ever written about that before we did.

Nobody had ever made that premise so clearly that every frustration an owner-operator experienced could be tied back to that fact—that faulty assumption.

We discovered that fact; we didn't make it up.

We discovered that fact by calling on them—small businesses—as a day-to-day reality of our business.

Our clients-to-be were not entrepreneurs. They were technicians who thought of their business as a job—NOT a future enterprise.

Our Job was to fix that problem.

Our Job was to inspire them to see the truth—about their companies, about their mindset, about their frustrations—that, at the root of it, was preventing their ability to scale, to grow, to expand beyond being a rough-and-tumble, mom-and-pop business.

Our Job was to first teach them how to turnkey their Job.

That was their underlying problem, and our underlying opportunity.

At the Heart of the Job

This discovery—the concept of the entrepreneurial seizure, and the turnkey solution to their frustrations—was an epiphany for many of our seminar attendees. They felt the truth in the concept (as did we), but needed to see how it was applied in the real world—and they needed to see it applied to our own small business if we were to be seen legitimately as the providers of their solution.

When we were going door-to-door asking questions, we'd established ourselves as "a business development firm" on the search for "why most small businesses don't work and what to do about it."

We didn't pretend to be that; we were intent upon being that.

That was our Dream, our Vision, our Purpose, and our Mission.

So, we needed to invent a core operating system as our Client Fulfillment System.

And we needed to design, build, launch, and grow that system in a very special way. Not so Tom and I could do it. But so that others— Mary and Jerry and Jimmy—could do it.

And not because Mary and Jerry and Jimmy were business development experts. But exactly the opposite; because they weren't!

Which was core to our position in the marketplace.

In order to achieve that objective of ours, we had to set out to do for ourselves the very same thing we were imploring our clients-to-be to do.

We had to invent the scalable, universal business development SYSTEM, which could have resonance with and be applied to every single small business on the planet, and (in our own application) be delivered by our minimum wage, no-experience coaches, in exactly the same way every single time—in the same way a Big Mac is made.

Like the very best system is made. To be scalable. To be replicable. To be manageable. To be repeatable. To follow the quality lexicon and to flawlessly and consistently exhibit its best practices, delivering a consistent, satisfying result.

And to accomplish that, we (and they) had to build our "franchise prototype." ✤

THE FIRST PART OF YOUR FRANCHISE PROTOTYPE

. . . serendipity is when you're looking for something and you find something else that's even better . . . Synchronicity is when two independent variables happen at the same time, in a pseudo-meaningful way. Serendipity is scientific, synchronicity isn't.

—Michael Gruber, *Tropic of Night*

So, all of the work you've been doing, calling on your most important customer, over and over again, is only done if it is ultimately addressing the most critical result of this process: getting to truly know your customer.

For us, that's what happened following the Key Frustrations Seminar.

We gave each of the attendees an opportunity to complete a FREE Needs Analysis of their company.

The needs analysis was designed to walk our potential customer through a process, a checklist, which itemized every single system any business needed to have, in Marketing, Operations, Finance, Human Resources, Administration, and Sales.

As with everything we did from those earliest development days—from the cold call, to the invitation to attend our seminar, to the seminar itself—the Needs Analysis Process was fully scripted from start to finish.

To deliver a Needs Analysis, our Senior Marketing Associate needed to memorize that script, and follow it precisely.

There were six benchmarks in the process.

- The first benchmark was to assure our Senior Marketing Associate that the owner-operator she was leading through the analysis got the point of The Key Frustrations Seminar.

- The second was to establish that his or her business wasn't the problem—the owner-operator was the problem.

- The third was to clarify exactly why he or she was the problem

- The fourth was to confirm an understanding that the owner-operator was not truly an entrepreneur, but a technician suffering from an entrepreneurial seizure.

- The fifth was to reach an agreement that it was killing him.

- The sixth was to explain that the purpose of the Needs Analysis was to discover how badly it was killing him, by identifying what was missing in his company—the systems that weren't there.

Which, when taken in total, described what we called "the gap" between where the company was today in relationship to where it COULD be if he were to approach the development of his company exactly as Ray Kroc did with McDonald's.

It could then become a discussion about putting the systems in place so it could scale.

Key to getting to that point from our Needs Analysis Process—which was, itself, a rigorous turnkey system—was that the benchmarks were followed scrupulously. You didn't go to Benchmark Two until you had successfully completed Benchmark One. You didn't go to Benchmark Three until you had successfully completed Benchmark Two. And so forth.

There was a powerful and elegant dual result of what some beginning Marketing Associates may have at first seen as an overly rigid adoption of our system of scripting and benchmarks:

By adhering to our systems, and experiencing the success of the intended results, our people came to believe at a more heartfelt level in our point of view—in the story they were telling our small business owners—as they became witnesses to the literal magic of the McDonald's model for small business development and extreme growth.

In other words, by literally practicing what it is we had declared from the onset was the key to the success of our clients' businesses, they 1) demonstrated a "live" version of "the system"; 2) experienced, by so doing, its impact on their client as well as themselves; and 3) reinforced the truth of the contention—our model and promise.

The message conveyed was simple and compelling: That unless and until you, a small business owner, completely adopted systems thinking as the core operating reality of your company, your company would never grow—not successfully so–and all you would be creating for yourself is a job. A job that only you can do. A job that only you would be crazy enough to do.

The core of the needs analysis was the Key Frustrations Checklist.

Walking through the Checklist with the prospective client identified the missing pieces in his or her small business puzzle—which, in turn, were the systems that needed to be there, but were not.

That Checklist was an eye opener and an emotional roller coaster.

Using the script and mindful of the benchmarks, our Senior Marketing Associate walked her prospective client patiently through the Checklist, asking the questions: "Do you have this? Do you have that? Do you know this? Do you know that?" From function to function to function to function. It became transparently clear that our prospective client didn't have almost anything he or she needed to have in order to operate his or her company as effectively as Ray Kroc did his.

THE MEASURE OF THE MODEL

In our seminar, we established the measure we were going to use throughout our process of establishing our credibility, and challenging the small business owners we were calling on.

And that "gap"—the sum and total of those missing pieces we revealed in the needs analysis—was the measure.

This was critical!

From the very outset, our credibility was always in question.

Just like yours is.

Just like mine is.

Just like every human being's is.

And your credibility is measured according to the model you're using.

So, if there isn't a model you're using, or if the model you're using is suspect, or if you haven't yet discovered the underlying problem that exists in your most important customer's life, or job, or business, or marriage, or relationship with money, or what have you, upon which to build your model—as every successful company must establish— you fail.

You fail because you have failed to establish a CONTEXT for your potential relationship with your most important customer.

And it's that CONTEXT for your relationship, not the CONTENT— and the verifiable TRUTH underlying it—which stands at the heart of your Client Fulfillment System when that system is finally done.

All of which is magnified, verified, and confirmed as you walk your prospective client through your Checklist (whatever systemic form for you that takes).

The Checklist, with the responses and answers you accumulate, is at the heart of your credibility, which is at the heart of the Story you will tell, which is at the heart of your Client Fulfillment System.

Because it is your Client Fulfillment System which is intended to solve that multiplex problem, by awakening (in the example of our client) the requirement–the absolute requirement if her company is to grow–to go to work ON her company, rather than just IN her company, to design, build, launch, and grow the essential systems which are needed in order to replicate her company's ability to produce the results it has promised to do.

All of what I've just shared with you is key to the development of your Client Fulfillment System, which says, quite simply: "This is how we do it here!" And nobody, but nobody does it as well.

How Do I Do That?

Which brings us to the obvious question: "How do I do that?"

"How do I create those systems, when I'm not sure what's needed in order to solve my most important customer's most important problem?"

The answer is simple.

You ask the question I shared above: "What's missing in this picture?"

Your Job isn't to give him or her the answer to the frustrations he or she has.

Your Job is to help him or her DISCOVER the answer to the main underlying problem they have.

Your Job is to help them identify their gap.

If it's software you're selling, IT does that.

If it's a service you're selling, IT does that.

If it's a soft drink you're selling, IT does that.

If it's printing, or photography, or copywriting, or carpentry, or architecture, or dentistry, or, well, anything, you're selling, IT does that.

IT MUST DO THAT!

Because if IT DOESN'T do that, they will go someplace else to buy it.

So, the process you're inventing, called your Client Fulfillment System, is going to be designed just as the process I shared with you above . . . your equivalent of the research cold call, the questioning, the booking for the seminar, the seminar itself, the scheduling of a needs analysis, the needs analysis itself, the Agreement the client signs, the Business Development Program we then delivered to our clients, and so forth . . . that entire process, with all its pieces and parts, is what I'm calling the Client Fulfillment System, from the very beginning to the very end.

Obviously, the pieces, the benchmarks, the steps and processes to your Client Fulfillment System may be entirely different from mine—but the framework, form, function, and intention is the same: to obtain a predictable and desired result for your client that is defined by, and in context with, the model you've identified—i.e., the compelling promise you made to your prospective client at the very beginning of your first contact with them.

And in its own unique way, it is visual, emotional, functional and financial, every single step of the way.

The Client Fulfillment System is your first step toward creating and validating the effectiveness of your Franchise Prototype.

Let's go on to look at the second and third step: Your Client Acquisition System. ✤

WHAT HAVE WE GOT SO FAR?

Given the right circumstances, from no more than dreams, determination, and the liberty to try, quite ordinary people consistently do extraordinary things.

—Dee Hock, *Birth of the Chaordic Age*

Before we proceed to Part Three of this book, and begin to look at your Client Acquisition System, let's stop, take a couple of deep breaths, review where we've been, and remember what we're doing here.

We're working ON your Company of One to build it step by step so that it operates with clarity, precision, and jubilation, to produce a Great Result for your customer-client.

In Part I, we addressed the <u>four categories of entrepreneurship</u>:

- Your Dream

- Your Vision

- Your Purpose

- Your Mission

We identified the <u>four personalities comprising an entrepreneur</u>:

- Your Dreamer

- Your Thinker

- Your Storyteller

- Your Leader

Your Dreamer has a <u>Dream</u>.

Your Thinker has a <u>Vision</u>.

Your Storyteller has a <u>Purpose</u>.

Your Leader has a <u>Mission</u>.

We discovered, at least superficially, your Dream, Vision, Purpose, and Mission, which translate into and direct the focus, energy, and supreme outcome you're determined to produce.

You started with "a blank piece of paper and beginner's mind" to create what I'm calling NewCo, rather than OldCo, which would be the company you've somehow created through whatever happenstance ruled your day-to-day activity up until now.

We said, and agreed, that until or unless you do that necessary work, that work in your Dreaming Room, you will fail to establish the platform for the work at hand, which is to invent your Great Growing Company to scale.

We determined that, ultimately, your <u>most</u> important customer is the one who's going to *buy* your company, as opposed to the one who's going to buy your product.

So, in that sense, your company IS your most important product.

And if your company hasn't the ability to scale—to grow, exponentially—it hasn't the wherewithal to be sold for its maximum potential value. It's not an Enterprise; it's just a shop—prettied up to sell to *another* technician, looking to own a job.

Remember, our job together is to go to work ON NewCo to design, build, launch, and grow it—to turnkey it—so that it possesses the profoundly unique ability it needs to scale.

Once that is a certainty—once your company *is* built to scale—the sale of your company is a certainty.

In **Part II,** we introduced the process for going to work ON your <u>Job</u>.

The first step in creating your Franchise Prototype was to design, build, launch, and grow your <u>Client Fulfillment System</u>.

This represents the core capability of your company to deliver what it is you're committed to deliver—your Dream, Vision, Purpose, and Mission—in a consistent, replicable, heartily effective manner, assuring for yourself, and your customer-client, that it is exactly what you say it is, and that it will always be so, such that your incomparable results will be constant and irreducible.

In short, you have examined every aspect of how you do what you do to deliver the promised results to your clients. You've identified and closed the gaps in that process. And you've captured and codified, or systematized, that process in such a way that it is proven, and foolproof, and you can point to that system with pride, declaring: "This is how we do it here!"

So, now, let's move on to **Part III:** Your Client Acquisition System. ✤

PART III

STRUMMING THE CHORDS OF THE MUSIC

"Your arrows do not carry," observed the Master, "because they do not reach far enough spiritually."

—Eugen Herrigel, *Zen and the Art of Archery*

This third section discusses the critical process of Your Client Acquisition System. Once created, fortified, and in place, this process will assure you that every single producer in your ready-to-grow company will have a sufficient number of client-customers to keep them busy, delivering what they have been trained to deliver—what you've promised—with incomparable, consummate consistency, joy, and skill.

Considered in another way, this means that you will then possess the ability to replicate the number of producers you wish to grow in your company to serve the number of client-customers you intend to serve through your company, and you will be able to produce those results at will.

Which means, ultimately, you will own and control the remarkable capability to replicate yourself with people possessing the consummate, required skills.

A Brief Thought on the Order of Things:

Throughout the years of my professional life, I have maintained a stubbornly held contention that flies, seemingly, in the face of what many have insisted is the rightful order of things in the development of a business. They say: "The order in which you need to get started is 1) come up with the product; 2) market it—in other words— figure out how to and begin trying to sell it; and 3) as the orders come in, figure out how to deliver it—one way or another."

My contention (as this book, my first book, and all the books in between have all instructed) has always been that they've got the order critically wrong for a business that intends to succeed beyond what may be an initial flash of unique visitors.

I would maintain that the order in which you develop your new company (NewCo) would be this: 1) come up with the product (Your Dream); 2) determine what it is you want your best customers to experience with your product—the impact you intend your product to have on their lives (Vision, Purpose, and Mission); then, 3) design and capture the process through which you will deliver or provide that experience and impact (Your Client Fulfillment System), and then, finally, 4) design, capture, and launch how you're going to attract potential customers to this company providing this experience.

In other words, "Production and Delivery" before "Marketing and Sales."

Counterintuitive?

Could be, but consider it this way:

It doesn't matter how successful you may be in marketing and sales (Client Acquisition) if you can't deliver on the promise your customers-to-be perceive to be your promise-to-be.

You get only one chance to get it right. One chance to not disappoint. One chance to demonstrate absolute confidence, elegance, seamlessness, and consistency in delivering your promise. If you provide anything less, your customers will be one-shot encounters—and unwilling to repeat the risk after they've been disrespected by your unpreparedness to serve them as they expected from your marketing.

Maybe call it the curse of good marketing.

The idea of "build it and they will come" is perfectly fine—because it assumes that it has, in fact, been built! It wasn't "get them in here and we'll figure it out."

So, why Client Acquisition after Client Fulfillment?

Simply put: If you (or your people) cannot completely, unabashedly, consistently, fully, proudly, and unreservedly deliver exactly what you promised to those best customers lined up in front of your counter in your first day of business, how dare you invite or encourage anyone else to walk through your door?

Client Acquisition is a process that begins with Lead Generation and ends with Lead Conversion.

However, to reduce it to just the mechanics, as most of us do, is to miss the point entirely.

The point of Client Acquisition is *not* to make a sale.

The point of Client Acquisition is to make a true believer.

And to make a true believer, you've got to address, communicate, share, and inspire an already overloaded audience to believe in something they don't want to believe in. They are skeptical to the core. They are cynical—and for good reason. They've been lied to by everybody. Most of all, they've lied to themselves. So, they don't believe in the other—the politician, the salesperson, the supposed leader, the judge, the jury, the cop, justice, the American Dream, the Priest, the Minister, the Rabbi, the Imam, and they don't believe in themselves. So it's going to take something irrefutably remarkable to help them switch gears.

You are that gear switcher.

If you're going to grow, that is.

And your Client Acquisition System is the lever you're going to use to accomplish that.

I call it "the music"—and it comes from your Storyteller.

Your Storyteller is going to have to learn how to capture your lyrics, compose your music, orchestrate your composition, sing your song, to tell a Story beyond the mundane and from the farthest reaches of the musical sphere, if it's ever going to be believed and taken home.

Because to be believed, it's got to be felt.

And to be felt it's got to touch both one's heart and one's mind.

And for that to happen, it has to *originate* in one's heart and one's mind.

Let's take a look at a great Story. ❧

Part III: Chapter Ten

A GREAT STORY

Stories are the creative conversion of life itself into a more powerful, clearer, more meaningful experience. They are the currency of human contact.

—Robert McKee

At the heart of your Client Acquisition System is a Great Story.

And that Great Story is what fueled the creation of your Client Fulfillment System.

Understand that your Client Fulfillment System is both the genesis of your Client Acquisition System, and the outcome of your discovery of it.

Your Client Fulfillment System is the product of your Dream, Vision, Purpose, and Mission. As is your Client Acquisition System.

Meaning, while they appear to be two—Client Fulfillment, Client Acquisition—they are actually one.

It's that singular fact that takes you beyond the ordinary to be in a position to discover the extraordinary.

And that's what's at the heart of a Great Story.

The fact that it is one. A Great Growing Company is one.

When you look down upon your company from above—from a strategic perspective—it is nothing but One Great Thing.

AND THE STORY GROWS FROM WITHIN:

Allow me to share a story about that from Awakening the Entrepreneur Within, *Chapter 18: Page 143: "And the Story Grows from Within."*

I want to create a world of meaning. I want to contribute to that by inventing a new business prototype that will exceed anything I have ever done. It will do what it does exactly as I perceive it. It will be a business of meaning. It will produce cash flow from the very beginning in excess of what it costs to produce that cash flow. This business I am inventing will make a demonstrable difference in people's lives. I will make that difference the point of my Story. My Story will describe that business to a T. People will say when they hear my Story, "Wow, how do you do that?" And I will tell them exactly how we do that. But even more important, I will tell them why we do that. My Story will get better and better each time I tell it. It will become the passion that fuels my life. I will see myself as a leader in the world of people making a difference in the world. I will seek out those people who make a difference in the world to tell them my Story, and to ask them to tell me theirs. I will seek out great Stories every day and in every way possible. I will build a personal library of great Stories and read one of them at the beginning of every day and at the end of every day to fuel my life with their passion. I am a writer of great Stories. I believe in the power of great Stories. I believe in the power of great Stories as they are told by great teachers of great Stories. I am dedicated to becoming a great author of my great Story and a great teacher of great Stories, mine and every other great teacher's great Story. I live to inspire human beings to live great lives. I am committed to the Path of Greatness not for myself, but for those who will be profoundly affected by it. For those who will follow me on that path. For those who are hurting for want of a great Story, a great path, a great calling. I will create such a great path, such a great Story, such a great calling as I write my great Story, as I invent my great path. I envision a world of great warriors. Inner warriors, not outer warriors. Inner warriors who are equally committed to the Great Path. Inner warriors who are committed to leading the Great Life. Inner warriors who are committed to write their great Story, to tell their great Story, to create their great path, to live the great life, the life of a great warrior. I have written this for you. I have invited you with this book to join me in the creation of my great Story by creating your great Story as we all create the great story of all Stories of all time. The world will never be the same, brothers and sisters. The world will not challenge us. The world will greet us, harbor us, feed us, nurture us, and inspire us, because the world is a great Story—the greatest Story of all.

So, if all that is true, then what? Let's take it apart together.

Your promise touches their heart, their soul, their imagination, their perceived needs—*their life*—in a way no one else has and does.

AT THE HUB OF A GREAT STORY

At the hub of a Great Story is something which no one has spoken about before.

Or, better said, no one has spoken about it the way you are intent upon speaking about it.

If you look at the internet marketing frenzy of the past decade, you'll immediately see what I mean.

Info marketers galore.

All of whom have been practicing their industry's info-marketing rules, which have been developed by those very same info marketers as they practice their info-marketing art, science, black magic, and craft upon you.

There has been a substantial array of info-marketing tomes written on the subject.

And, if you're having difficulty discovering the books you should read, or the info-marketing guru you should follow, Google lists three hundred and thirty-one million (331,000,000!) opportunities for you to become an info-marketing wizard . . . There is an info-marketing association. There are info-marketing groups by the tens of thousands. There are thousands of info-marketing Mastermind Groups. There are thousands of info-marketing Meetups. There are info-marketing gurus galore. Folks you've never heard of, and folks you supposedly should have heard of. There are info-marketing coaches, info-marketing mentors, info-marketing trainers, and info-marketing services . . . more than I can or would list here . . . not because they might steal you away from these pages, but simply because until you get to the heart of the subject—at the heart of client acquisition—all of that stuff will take you down a rabbit hole you'll never come out of. And I mean exactly that, never!

So, we're not going down that rabbit hole, because as entertaining as it could be, when we're done, you would sound exactly like everyone else pursuing the very same thing: the secret underlying info marketing. And the secret underlying info marketing resides solely in the process we're engaged in here.

And that's because Client Acquisition is not the technology of it, it's the context of it. Meaning, you must hit the heart of your client-customer's raw spot, and you must do so in language that uncovers the *need*.

Your need, for example, is that you've not yet discovered how to speak about why you're in the business you're in in a way that differentiates you from everyone else in the very same business.

And the reason for that is you've never before thought about it in the way I'm about to describe it to you here.

You've thought about it in terms of <u>sales</u>—meaning, in terms of your company and what it needs—rather than in terms of transformation—meaning, the potential transformation of your customer-client's life.

Client Acquisition is Client Fulfillment in the fullest meaning of the phrase.

You acquire a customer-client because, and only because, your story touches them at the heart of their greatest need. ✤

A FEW SEMINAL THOUGHTS

Begin as a creation, become a creator. Never wait at a barrier. In this kitchen stocked with fresh food, why sit content with a cup of warm water?

—Jalal ad-Din Muhammad Rumi

There is a process that lives within a Great Story, and I'll suggest what that process is. But, it is only a suggestion.

Begin by knowing this: no one can tell you how to write a Great Story.

Not I.

Not anyone.

Despite the fact that there are many who will tell you they can.

But the moment you follow any process as suggested, your Story will end up being simply a rehash of what others have told you are the ingredients of a Great Story. And those ingredients, I can promise you, will create something significantly less than a truly Great Story.

The very best book I've ever read about the Story, Robert McKee's, *Story: Substance, Structure, Style, and the Principles of Screenwriting,* tells it most clearly.

In his Introduction, McKee lays out, not rules—he doesn't believe in rules—but principles.

McKee says:

> *"Story is about principles, not rules."*

> *"Story is about eternal, universal forms, not formulas."*

> *"Story is about archetypes, not stereotypes."*

> *"Story is about thoroughness, not shortcuts."*

> *"Story is about realities, not the mysteries of writing."*

> *"Story is about mastering the art, not second-guessing the marketplace."*

> *"Story is about respect, not disdain, for the audience."*

> *"Story is about originality, not duplication."*

If you're truly serious about writing your Great Story, I would recommend you read McKee's great book.

I would further recommend you select some of the greatest stories ever written, or ever told. Think back to some you've read or heard;

why have they stayed with you? They needn't have been classics (although there are certainly many of McKee's principles to be found in books that have become "classics").

Re-read them, recall stories told to you, and hear them again; take notes as you do; dig into them to capture the essence of them.

One thing you'll find in every one of them is that in the heart of a Great Story—and a Great Storyteller—lies authenticity.

The author or the storyteller is consumed with his or her story. So much so that there is often little distinction between the writer and the storyteller.

When you begin this process of writing your Great Story, you begin it with less structure than is needed as you pursue it through its gyrations. Don't worry at all about structure, or grammar, or too much (or too little) detail.

That's what I speak of when I say, "a blank piece of paper and beginner's mind."

A Great Story starts wherever it starts and goes wherever it goes, until it begins to find its own form. Don't hesitate to let it ramble, go off on tangents and flights of fancy. It'll find its way back home. In fact, the more you write, the better lit will be the path.

You begin with that "blank sheet of paper and beginner's mind"—wholly permitting yourself to appreciate that you are creating a "first draft."

Its form is the form it must take as it reveals itself.

A Great Story, remember, is written for the reader, for the listener, for the viewer, for the audience, not for the author or The Storyteller.

The author of a Great Story is always judged by the reader, the listener, the viewer, the audience, not the author.

The author of a Great Story can fall in love with his Story, but after all that hugging and kissing and loving is done, the Story is still left in the hands of the reader, the listener, the viewer, the audience, not the author, as the Story is either going to fall in love with them, and them with it, or not. And if not, it doesn't matter how deeply infatuated you are with your Story, it will not be a Great Story. In the end, the Great Story and its reader, listener, viewer, audience, are embedded with each other or they're not.

In other words, ultimately, it is the reader or audience who declares the Great Story. If that fails to occur, it's just words conspired (often self-evidently) to persuade or manipulate—not move.

It's just commerce.

And if it's just commerce, shame on the author. Not because he is not great himself, but because he didn't care enough about his reader, listener, viewer, or audience to stick it out there.

Remember, sticking it out there is the great and impersonal redeemer for every great author.

STICKING IT OUT THERE – FROM *AWAKENING THE ENTREPRENEUR WITHIN*, 2008:

Do you truly recognize the liberation of it? We have just at this moment come to the inescapable, unavoidable, irrepressible joyful truth of it ... that with little more than a Great Idea, a Great Business

Model, and a Great Story, you can conceive, design, build, perfect, and roll out your own McDonald's—your own perfectly wonderful, meaningful Enterprise, and you can start doing it today with your own powerful Mission. The System is already there, my friend! And it's turnkey. All you need to do is apply it to your Great Idea, persist as you lead it forward, do as I have, and as so many millions of others have, are, and will. It's time to create a revolutionary new world. Go back now to the beginning, dear reader. Go back to all of your notes. Begin taking yourself seriously. Now that you see how simple this is going to be, go back and read your Great Story. Didn't write it yet? Then begin. Now. Before you forget how easy this is. Do you see that there is no longer any reason that you can't do it? It is not the money any longer. You can make the money as you go. It is not your inexperience any longer. You don't need any experience to create a remarkable new company. I didn't have any. Steve Jobs didn't have any. Bill Gates didn't have any. The Google boys didn't have any, nor did Martha Stewart, Debbie Fields, or Ben & Jerry. Almost no one who starts a business has any experience at all. So you don't need any business experience, either. All you need is a Dream. A Vision. A Purpose. A Mission. All you need is a Great Idea inspired by Passion; educated by your life; trained by whatever it was that taught you whatever you know; coached by those who cared about you when you needed direction; and mentored by Love. You've got everything you need to start, and that's where you are right now. At the start. Realize that this is not first about starting a business. No. Your business isn't the Start-up. You are the Start-up. The Start-up is You! If you had any doubts before this, the road now is clear ahead! Come dream with me, dear reader. Because we haven't even begun this great thing yet.

Sticking it out there is what the Storyteller must be compelled to do, if his Dream, Vision, Purpose, and Mission are to be honored to the degree a Great Story demands they be honored.

So, why do we speak of all this in such seemingly exalted terms?

Weren't we supposed to be on the topic of selling?

Isn't this Story thing just about business?

Isn't this Story thing just about getting somebody to buy something?

Isn't this Story thing just about getting on with it, getting on with making some money, getting stuff, living the good life, getting what you want, living the life you don't have?

Isn't this Story thing just about making it?

Well, yes, but most prodigiously, no.

Because at the deep and loving heart of creation, of doing the extreme work that a Disney did, a Jobs did, a Kroc did—as Musk or Branson or Schultz are doing—is much, much more than just business.

Indeed, not one of them, as outrageously successful as they were or are, was truly interested in business.

You might say, to be fair, to be brashly honest, they were each moved by what they might have called "the Spirit"—the stunning awakening that occurred within them as they pursued their craft.

The product of each—the companies they created—inspired their audience, their viewers, their readers, their listeners, their users, their fans and followers and employees in ways far beyond the ordinary. Their creations and enterprises have moved far beyond the simple reality of what they produced. Their creations are iconic, standing out as true originals. Their creations became something far, far more profound than the actual substance of them.

Kroc didn't just create hamburgers.

Jobs didn't just create computers.

Disney didn't just create cartoons, movies, entertainment.

Sir Richard Branson didn't just create an airline.

Howard Schultz didn't just buy a coffee shop.

The Stories they each created lived uniquely within the hearts and imaginations of their audiences.

As your Story will.

Should you take it as seriously as they did?

A Great Story lives within the truth it reveals.

What is the truth your Great Story is determined to reveal?

Let's look a little deeper. ❧

THE TRUTH YOUR GREAT STORY REVEALS

A business is simply an idea to make other people's lives better.

—Sir Richard Branson

The truth your Great Story reveals is always about what's missing in this picture.

And what's missing in this picture is essential if this picture—the life of your most important client-customer—is going to be fulfilled.

That is the truth your Great Story is going to reveal.

What's missing, why it's missing, the price your viewer, reader, listener, audience is paying because of the absence of what's missing, and what must absolutely happen for that "missingness" to be filled.

That's what happens when your Great Story realizes its potential greatness—that missingness must be filled.

It's what happens when a great orator speaks his or her mind.

It's what happens when the Great Story, the truth of things, is expressed with the force it deserves, and demands, and requires for you, the Storyteller, to capture the heart and mind of your dearly intended.

What you say, and how you say it, must envelop the consciousness of those in attendance.

It must say to them: "Listen to me for this is real!"

It must say to them: "Listen to me because if you miss what I'm about to share with you, the absence of my message will continue to take its toll on you, as it has up until this very moment!"

Your Great Story must reveal what has never been revealed, and, despite the fact that your audience has never heard anything like your Great Story before, they will, the majority of them, understand that it is revealing the real, the true, the essential. Not to everyone—but to them. It is deeply personal. It is emphatic. It is beyond question fundamental to living the true life, the one they have been given to live.

Your Great Story is always about going beyond the ordinary, going beyond the mere stuff that goes on every day—beyond the mere commerce of it, the mere money of it, the mere doing of it, the mere living of it, or the mere endurance of it.

Your Great Story must always rise above the reality everyone experiences, so far beyond it that the discomfort it creates—and if it's doing its job, it will always create discomfort—will put your audience into an internally indigestible uncomfortable space.

That has always happened as I shared my Great Story with the tens of thousands of business people I've shared it with over the past 40 years.

It might even be happening right now with you.

That discomfort created by the incongruence of what's going on in your mind right now, and what you were led to expect at the outset of this Story, that this is a book about business.

That business doesn't sound like the Story I'm telling you right now.

It doesn't, does it?

Just like the fire walk Tony Robbins invites his audiences to take.

That kind of discomfort.

Like the Great Discomforter, Werner Erhard, took his hundreds of thousands of EST students through in the face of his Great Story.

The Great Story that lies at the heart of Zen.

The Great Story that lives at the heart of Disney's Imagineering.

"Don't bring me what you know," Disney said to his Imagineers, "bring me what you've never done or seen before."

The Great Story upon which the iMac was created.

The Great Story upon which Netflix was created.

The Great Story, for that matter, upon which the Torah was created, where on Mount Sinai Moses was handed the tablets which he brought down to the Jewish people.

The Great Story is the Great Story and nothing less than that.

You'll know it when it reveals itself to you.

But, it won't reveal itself to you if you're not actively and consciously in search of it.

The energy of the search is not sufficient to discover your Great Story, but you will not find your Great Story without that great energy being expended.

It won't just come to you in a few moments of meditation or determination.

It will only come to you when you take your audience more seriously than you take yourself.

This is heavy lifting I'm talking about.

This is Spiritual work.

This is the work of the extreme logician, the seeker, the seer—well outside the comfort zone.

And if you're not comfortable with that level of discomfort, too bad. It's a given in this work.

I've been around this kind of work for decades, since I was a kid learning how to master the saxophone, or, a bit older, learning how to sell encyclopedias, learning how to frame a house, learning how to do the Work of Gurdjieff, learning how to find the inner child, learning how painful it is to fail and to pick myself back up again.

Learning how to lead and watching everyone go the other way.

Learning how unbearable it is to discover how stupid I can be.

Learning how painful it is to misunderstand marriage, divorce, love and estrangement, and learning how to lose myself and find my way again.

That's the stuff of the Great Story.

That's what I'm suggesting you need to take on, as Gurdjieff was wont to say, "whole hog plus the postage," and that you have absolutely no choice in the matter.

That's your responsibility as you awaken the entrepreneur within.

If you choose to.

And even if you don't.

So, having said that, let's take a very quick look at the mechanics of it.

And then get on with the extreme growth of your Business.

And the revelation of your turnkey Management System. ✤

THE MECHANICS OF IT

Precision instruments are designed to achieve an idea, dimensional precision, where perfection is impossible. There is no perfectly shaped part of the motorcycle and never will be, but when you come as close as these instruments take you, remarkable things happen, and you go flying across the countryside under a power that would be called magic if it were not so completely rational in every way.

—Robert M. Pirsig, *Zen and the Art of Motorcycle Maintenance*

The mechanics of Client Acquisition are straightforward.

First there's Lead Generation.

Then there's Lead Conversion.

You first want to attract folks to you.

And then there's the process of converting them into a Customer.

Once you've converted them into a Customer, the mechanics of Client Fulfillment converts them into a lasting Client.

There are, I think, a few important things to keep in mind when thinking about these systems, and I present them here with the suggestion that all, in combination, can lead to a more precise way of thinking about and subsequently building, launching, and growing your Client Acquisition System:

- Lead Generation has a distinct and definable beginning, middle, and end; it begins in your first efforts to identify your best customer—who they are, where they are, and what needs they hope to fill. Your Lead Generation System ends at the point at which a potential customer identifies themselves as such—they raise their hand, send an email inquiry, click for more information, make a phone call, walk into your shop and ask a question. They are, at that point, a generated lead.

So it follows that all of your efforts in Lead Generation (and all of your measurements and quantifications to evaluate your system's effectiveness) revolve around and are limited to those efforts that end in someone saying: "Tell me more."

- Lead Conversion begins directly after that point of first attraction, is marked by all the specific, progressive steps that would follow (generally confirming the need and offering the solution), and ends, of course, with your interested prospect deciding to do business with you, placing an order for your product or service.

Just as with Lead Generation, there are a number of benchmarks and measurements you'll want to routinely capture (as part of your system) to be perpetually evaluating the effectiveness of your Lead Conversion efforts.

Following Lead Conversion, of course, is Client Fulfillment—and your Client Fulfillment System was, you'll recall, the very first system you developed. It should make increasing sense to you why that would have been the order of things; putting it bluntly, knowing with all of your heart and mind that you have in place an iron-clad ability to do what you're promising, will, if nothing else (and there is much more), increase your connection with your client-to-be, in your being able to express your complete assurance and confidence in your ability to make and keep the promise they're seeking.

And before we leave this, let me say one more thing about this wonderful network of primary systems.

And that is, that they are clearly interrelated and interdependent, and ought to be constantly synchronizing and recalibrating with one another; and that also, they should not be thought of as strictly linear.

In other words, once the initial notice has been achieved by someone who thinks they might be interested in what you have, all of these three systems start working together, rather like a single organism, but with separate and distinct responsibilities—all leading to the same goal.

Put simply, consider the fact that from the very first time your prospective customers get a whiff of awareness of your existence and, therefore, are systemically in your Lead Generation System, they are simultaneously having an experience of your Client Fulfillment System as well. Every impression, every action, every response, every exploratory click on your website or encounter with your answering system is a precursor to what they have every reason to believe will be their ultimate experience with your company.

You are, through your systems, sending messages and signals in all directions and at all levels to receivers (your prospective customers) who are more hyper-sensitive and highly tuned than at any other time in their relationship with you.

I mention this now, as we begin to shift our focus in Part IV to your Management System, as it is, of course, that system that may bear the primary responsibility, if not for designing or building your Client Acquisition System, then certainly for monitoring its effectiveness on an on-going basis to keep your operation staged for continuous growth. ✤

PART IV

PART IV

TAKING A STEP BACK

Whatever you can do or dream you can, begin it. Boldness has genius, magic and power in it. Begin it now.

—Goethe

Think of this chapter as a step backward so we can reconstitute our measure of agreement.

If you believe yourself to be completely in tune with what we've been discussing, that's fine.

But, work through this step with me, as I believe you'll discover something important here.

Something essential to the process of designing, building, launching, and growing your company to scale.

Remember, your company is the product you're creating to produce the legacy of your life. It is a lasting mark of your time here on earth.

It is your gift to the universe of which you are a part. This is the process we're engaged in.

I am of the belief that every human was born to create a legacy of their very own.

That even if we ignore it, we can't help but produce it.

The question is, and will always be, what is the value of it?

I am of the belief that for each of us our legacy is significantly bolder, bigger, brasher, more important, more meaningful, and more special than the one we are currently creating.

You see, I am of the belief that you are, and have been, since the day of your birth and currently, creating your legacy.

I am also of the belief that you don't do that intentionally.

Very few of us think in terms of legacy.

Instead, we think in terms of life and no life.

We live the life we live, and then we die. Which means, for most of us, then it's over.

We don't think about that a lot.

Because if we did think about that a lot, we, most of us, would get heartily depressed.

On the other hand, for most of us, our life isn't anything special.

That's why, I believe, personal growth mantras have gained so much popularity.

Those personal growth mantras and magicians (I think of them as M-squared) have fed into the fact that few of us feel our lives to be special, so we're readily available for someone who tells us something different.

It is the personal growth phenomenon which has created what is called the "Me Generation."

That jacked us up, and turned us out.

Indeed, if we were to believe the mantras of the "Me Generation" we would honestly come to believe that WE—the "ME" they're all talking about—actually DO believe our lives are special. That we deserve everything we can get. More so than ever before in the history of being human.

In reality, should you choose to look much, much closer, you'll find exactly the opposite to be true.

To most of us, WE, the "ME" they're all talking about, suck.

That our lives *aren't* special.

Not by a long shot.

Not even close.

That instead, our lives are trivial.

Indeed, that life *itself* is trivial.

That everything is going to come to a very trivial and catastrophic end.

Which is Why Your Legacy Is So Very, Very Important

You see, when you begin to focus your attention ON your life, rather than just IN your life—on *creating* your life, rather than just *living* your life—only then will you truly comprehend objectively, not just subjectively, why your life is so very, very important.

Your life is the product you were sent here to create.

You were born—we were all born—to create the world.

And the way we do that, create the world, is to go to work ON our lives, not just IN our lives, to invent our lives, in order to produce something of great and compelling value for the world.

That something of "great and compelling value" is what I am calling your *legacy.*

You can do that, working ON, as opposed to just working IN, no matter what you elect to do with your time.

You can do it on a job, on a for-profit or non-profit, or you can do it on a company of your own.

I'm suggesting in this book that there is nothing more powerful than doing it on a company of your own.

I'm suggesting that those individuals who start up their own company, with a mind to grow it, are best equipped to leave a great and enduring legacy . . . if they approach the process as we're describing it here.

That, in most cases, should you decide to create a company of your own *without* the legacy mindset, most often you'll produce something significantly less than what you have in mind—and what you don't.

It's thinking "legacy" that fine-tunes the process.

Thinking of the end game puts the power into the present game necessary to provide the essential momentum to take you to that profoundly important end game, which takes you to the meaningful importance of your legacy.

It's that momentum—think strategic momentum, not tactical—which pulls everything and everyone together.

It's that momentum that communicates your earnest strategic intention to everyone your company is designed to touch.

To your contractors, your employees, your partners, your associates, your customers, your clients, your community, your lenders, your investors, your family, your suppliers, your world.

Everyone in your life-streaming community is moved by your momentum, intelligently expressed.

Everyone, as well, is deflated by your lack of momentum, your lack of a higher purpose, your lack of passion, your lack of great intention and, so deflated, deflates what momentum you do have to become significantly less.

So, that's why so few small companies succeed.

That's why most small companies, if they do manage to grow, come face-to-face with the chaos which surrounds them, and, unprepared for it, shrink to fit. Shrink to get small again. Shrink to go back to doing it, doing it, doing it, busy, busy, busy again. Shrink to going back to a Company of One.

Let's look at that reality, the art of one's legacy, in the many ways it expresses itself on a day-to-day basis in your company, in your world.

THE VISUAL, EMOTIONAL, FUNCTIONAL, AND FINANCIAL COMPONENTS OF A LEGACY

Whether you choose to or not, you are inventing a world.

And the world you are inventing is a visual, emotional, functional and financial world.

Your company is an aggregate of those four essential components.

Whether you choose to accept that or not, it is a fact. Your company is an aggregate of those four essential components: visually, emotionally, functionally, and financially.

I met a former Marine, now an entrepreneur, and asked him what stood out most in his memory about "Semper Fi," about his Marine Corps experience.

I had an expectation, before I asked him that question, of what he would say.

I expected that he would remember the bold and dynamic meaning of the Corps, the camaraderie of his teammates, the dress code, the rigor of the discipline, the credo of the Corps, and the way in which they affected him and became a significant part of his life today as an entrepreneur.

He would miss the discipline, the connection with his "brothers" and how that played itself out in their day-to-day lives, and the battles they fought together.

Surprisingly, he said something quite different.

He said he didn't miss it at all.

I was astonished and, frankly, hugely disappointed.

Because when I looked at the Corps from the outside in, my impression was something quite different.

I saw how little of the dignity of their mission, the price they each were willing to pay for it, the sacrifice so many of them made to honor the Code, to honor their commitment to the country they served, could be found in most of my experiences here in "the real world."

To me, it was the dignity and honor of it that was most important if one were to design, build, launch, and grow a truly significant enterprise.

To me, it was the extreme absence of a Code, the extreme absence of a Corps, the extreme absence of the discipline and devotion that earmarked for me the extreme absence of a legacy at the core of most small businesses on the face of this earth.

Because in order for your Company of One to become a Company of 1,000, and to do so with intrinsic, deeply felt meaning, a Code is absolutely essential.

And that Code is visual, emotional, functional, and financial.

(I've written extensively about these four, mainly in my second book, *The Power Point*—written before there was such a thing known as a power point—and later in *The E-Myth Enterprise*. Should you wish to know more about how the visual, emotional, functional and financial play themselves out in the creation of a Great Growing Company, read them.)

Let me say here, that just as I was disappointed with my Marine's thoughts about what it meant to him, so have I been continuously disappointed with the extreme deflationary mindset inhabited by most small business owners I've met over the years.

My very first client, years ago, a plumber, put it most succinctly when he said in response to my enthusiasm about the possibility of transforming his plumbing firm:

"New ideas get old, Gerber."

That was it. That was the whole of it. That was the expression I've dealt with over the past 40 years, as my journey to "transform the state of small business worldwide" was greeted by the reality, "New ideas get old, Gerber"—so let's not have any more new ideas!

Which meant that Ray Kroc, and Steve Jobs, and Walt Disney, and all the rest of them be damned!

Nothing like that going on over here.

Which is why Steve Jobs, Ray Kroc, and Walt Disney did create a legacy. A legacy that continues to be celebrated by one and all.

A visual legacy. An emotional legacy. A functional legacy. A financial legacy.

Which is exactly what we're speaking about doing here.

So, let's get on with it.

We've now discussed your Job and its Client Fulfillment System and your Practice and its Client Acquisition System and Client Fulfillment System, and the way the two interact. We've now discussed the Dream, Vision, Purpose, and Mission which are driving it all. It's where the momentum comes from.

We're now ready to take the next and most profound step of all: replicating your Practice to grow your Business by designing, building, launching, and growing your turnkey Management System.

Let's do it. ❧

YOUR MANAGEMENT SYSTEM: A WORLD WITHIN A WORLD

To me the desire to create and to have control over your own life, irrespective of the politics and the time or the social structure, was very much part of the human spirit. What I did not fully realize was that work could open the doors to my heart.

—Dame Anita Roddick, *Body and Soul*

Your Practice is now built.

Your <u>Client Fulfillment System</u> has been designed, built, launched, and then grown, and it is working spectacularly.

Not only that, but you have documented all of it.

It's the book about "how we do it here," which you can be assured that anyone you hand that book off to, any technician at all, can not only understand it, but can actually perform from it, exactly as you have so successfully done.

Your <u>Client Acquisition System</u> has been designed, built, launched, and then grown as well, and it, too, is working spectacularly well.

And you have documented all of it.

It, too, is a book about "how we do it here," which you can also be assured that anyone you hand that book off to, any technician at all, can not only understand it, but can actually perform from it, exactly as you have so successfully done.

(I repeat these mantras again and again for a most important reason.)

While most people who have read my books are inspired by the lessons I've shared with them, only too quickly, given the monstrous amount of work they each have to do, they promptly forget what I said.

In short, despite the belief they have that they're going to do it, they don't do it. They just think about it instead.

And so, I repeat myself.

Hoping upon hope that the lessons I'm sharing with you will become integrated into your very being.

That you know these are the things you're going to do, not just think about.

That it's critical that you do do them.

And it's critical that you do do them simply because they work, exactly as I'm speaking about them. They have worked, and will continue to work if only you follow my prescriptions to the letter.

MY TEACHERS:

My saxophone teacher, in my youth, told me: "Practice for as LONG as I tell you to practice. Practice exactly WHAT I tell you to practice. Practice exactly HOW I tell you to practice. And you too will become—should you care to—one of the best saxophone players in the world."

Just like my encyclopedia sales manager told me: "MEMORIZE these words EXACTLY as they're laid out on the page. Speak these words exactly HOW I tell you to speak them. Speak these words as OFTEN as I tell you to speak them. And you too will become—should you care to—one of the best encyclopedia salesmen in the world."

Just like my home building master told me: "Frame this house EXACTLY as I show you to frame it. Allow your hammer to do what it does without forcing it with your arm. Practice exactly WHAT I'm telling you to practice, exactly HOW I'm showing you to practice. Put your mind and body to it exactly as I'm showing you to do it, and you too will become—should you care to—one of the best framers in the world."

These lessons of mine have been put to good work in each and every case.

But not just to become the best in the world, but to learn the nature of work and its relationship with outcomes; to learn the ingredients of living a masterful life.

My teachers have given me that.

And not one of them had met any of the others!

But, their lessons were identically the same!

Whether it be about playing the saxophone, or selling encyclopedias, or framing a house.

So it is with your Management System.

So it is with the core competency your company must possess.

So it is with creating a true legacy.

So it is with sharing what you've learned—by doing it—in your time here on earth.

But, remember, in each and every case, the caveat was explicit: "Should you care to."

"Should you care to" was the driving force behind every one of my teachers.

"Should you care to" was always there in my lessons.

"Should you care to" told me that my success wasn't up to the music, or up to the sales script, or up to the lessons I received on framing a house.

"Should you care to" put the entire exercise on me, not on them. On me, not on my teachers.

"Should you care to."

So let's get on with the Business, and your <u>Management System</u>. ❧

DOING BUSINESS vs OWNING A BUSINESS

The chief characteristic of the volitional act is the existence of a purpose to be achieved; the clear vision of an aim.

—Robert Assagioli, *The Act of Will*

In case you haven't realized it yet, the term "business" is almost always used incorrectly to name something which isn't a business. Not by a long shot.

Just because you're DOING business, doesn't mean you actually OWN a business.

Few actually so-called "business owners" actually do own a *business*.

Which begs the question then, what IS a business?

Let's look again at our definitions:

A Business is an aggregate of up to seven turnkey Practices, plus a turnkey Management System!

Did you get that? Please read it again so that it sinks deeply into your entrepreneurial consciousness:

A <u>Business</u> is an aggregate of up to seven turnkey <u>Practices</u>, plus a turnkey Management System!

Up to now, we've been looking at your Job and at your Practice, trying to fully appreciate the what, why, and how of your Client Fulfillment and Client Acquisition Systems.

Because if you don't do that—and fully appreciate why you're doing that— your Business, this very thing we're calling an aggregate of up to seven turnkey Practices plus a turnkey Management System, will never work, will never take off, will never possess the inherent ability it must possess to scale, to grow, and to be managed, expertly, decisively, effectively, masterfully!

But, once you DO invent your turnkey Client Fulfillment System and your turnkey Client Acquisition System, you're now ready to replicate them. To replicate them in exactly the same way that Ray Kroc replicated his McDonald's hamburger stand, or Schultz' Starbucks coffee shop, or Subway Sandwiches, or Walmart, or Apple, or H&R Block, or a distinguishing number of now well-known enterprises—most of which started as **Dreams,** became **Jobs,** solidified as **Practices,** then, with the ability to replicate in place, became **Businesses,** until, finally, those clusters or aggregates of businesses morphed and expanded into the globe-covering **Enterprises** they are today.

THE PICTURE ON THE BOX

So, by now you should have most certainly gotten the profound and simple-minded secret I've been sharing with you all this time, that the game of business is no mystery. It's a very clear and definable puzzle that rewards you with a clear picture when the pieces are put together.

And it's your job to determine, before you create the puzzle, what the picture is!

It's your job to paint that freaking picture, and then to cut out and examine all the little pieces that, when put together, reveal the picture you knew was there all the time!!!

That's what we did when we started this puzzle, way back there at the beginning.

We created a Dream, a Vision, a Purpose, and a Mission—the seeds of your Great Growing Company.

You might say, using the metaphor of the puzzle, your Dreaming outlined the broad strokes of your picture, the picture of your emerging Enterprise, so that you could then go to work ON your Job, to design, build, launch, and grow your Client Fulfillment System, which defined the key piece of your emerging Enterprise: your product—the deliverable everything else you do depends upon.

And once you created your Client Fulfillment System, the next most important thing you had to do was to create your Client Acquisition System so you could attract a continuing flow of truly fanatical hopefuls who stood up to say, "tell me more, tell me more, tell me more." And you told them more, to the point where they said, "count me in," and they bought what you were selling them, consistently, dependably, in the numbers necessary to produce a profit with every sale you made, and every service you delivered.

And they grew, and grew, and grew, justifying the expansion of your company, of your Practice, justifying the replication of your Practice, times two, times three, times four, and so on. And so, as your three-legged stool achieved the mathematical and physical balance it required to stand firmly on its own three legs, you came to the realization that, yes, indeed, you were now ready to grow. And that's how we came to this exceptional point in time.

This is where you're poised to grow your Business, by simply replicating, faithfully, the success of your very first Practice.

Managing the Business of Practices

To make the leap from a well-oiled Practice to a fully functioning Business made up of up to seven Practices, you are now called to create something new. This is something you haven't really needed up to this point.

You need a <u>turnkey Management System</u>.

Because without a turnkey Management System, everything you've worked so hard to design, build, launch, and grow up to this point will all come tumbling down. Without a turnkey Management System, the core operating system upon which growth depends—comprised of Lead Generation, Lead Conversion, and Client Fulfillment—crumbles in disarray, just like almost every small company you walk into every single day.

It is impossible to make too large a point of this: your turnkey Management System is the key to growth!

Because without management, and without your ability to turnkey it, everything spins out of control, the wheels come off the axles, the entire operation goes pear-shaped, and you're back to where you started—but in worse shape, because you're now conscious of what could be, as you stare down at all the disconnected and disjointed and misused puzzle pieces of your company that was going to be.

So let's look at the components of your turnkey Management System, how it works, and why it works, and why, unless it IS turnkey, it will always let you down. ✤

A FOUR-LEGGED STOOL

Success is liking yourself, liking what you do, and liking how you do it.

—Maya Angelou

Picture your Management System as a four-legged stool. The four legs are:

- Innovation

- Quantification

- Orchestration

- Continuous Improvement

Innovation is the discovery and application of new and better ways to get results. It's improving everything you do. It's the opposite of the status quo. It's continually looking for a better way.

What is "everything you do"?

It's every aspect of the three-legged stool of your Practice: Lead Generation, Lead Conversion, and Client Fulfillment, all systematized and tailored with the express purpose of manifesting your Dream, your Vision, your Purpose and your Mission.

Meaning that you've done the base work in recognizing, identifying, and structuring your Lead Generation, Lead Conversion, and Client Fulfillment Systems. Most businesses never get that far. But innovation suggests that no system is static.

INNOVATION KNOWS STUFF CHANGES

If there's a way of doing something, there's a better way of doing something.

Consider a couple of very basic scenarios:

- As you turn a part of a system over to one of your technicians to operate instead of doing it yourself, the first thing she notices the first time she uses it is that there is, in fact, a missing step. It's not that you skipped that step when you were in the job, but only that you had become so expert at the job (or so bored with it that you could do it in your sleep) that you simply skipped capturing a step in your system–assuming it was obvious (which, I can assure you, it rarely is!). Your technician brings this missing documented step to your attention, and BAM: Innovation occurs!

- Your Client Fulfillment System, when it was first implemented, included the guidelines for sending a follow-up letter to your client, confirming their order. It perfectly outlined the steps for formatting the letter, printing it out on your letterhead, folding it and putting into the addressed envelope and calculating the postage. And then everybody got fax machines. And then everybody got email and electronically endorsable PDFs. Over time, your follow-up letter system needed to be modified and edited in order to maintain your operational clarity and stunning consistency within your operation and for your customers. Innovation occurs!

In fact, the opportunity should exist (and your Management System should support) innovation at all times. Remember, "New gets old, Gerber"? A good Management (and Leadership) System reinforces the culture that encourages every single one of your people operating within your Business to be ever on the lookout for actions, steps, tweaks, and new discoveries that could contribute to the increased efficiency and profitability of the operation.

And, of course, with all that Innovation occurring within each of your Practices making up your Business, a turnkey Management System is critical for providing a funnel and clearinghouse for the best of the evolving practices to be integrated coherently into your full operation.

Proof Through Quantification

Obviously, and not surprisingly, not all innovation is good. "New Coke" anyone?

When people are engaged and trying stuff—with the purest of intentions–some tries don't work. One only has to review the histories of the development of any of the hugely successful enterprises cited in this book to find instances of bad decisions, errors, and omissions. It comes with the territory. But, the frequency and severity of those missteps, and the alacrity with which they are discovered and recovered, speaks to the strength (and weaknesses) of that business's Management System.

So how did they (or how do you) know if an innovation is successful?

How do you know that the supposed improvement you've made is, in fact, an improvement? By measuring the impact it has on your customer.

Quantification means measuring.

<u>Every system you create must have at least one way to measure intended results</u>. For example:

- In the case of Lead Generation, more customers respond positively to your Lead Generation ministrations.

- In the case of Lead Conversion, a greater percentage of your prospective customers become paying customers.

- In the case of Client Fulfillment, a greater percentage of your paying customers opt in for more of what you're selling, or more of what you've included in your deliverables, beyond what they're buying at the present time. Secondarily, you may see a trending up-tick of referrals.

So it is that quantification is a critical leg of your turnkey Management System.

ORCHESTRATION: COMMITTING IT TO FORM

As your quantification tells you that you've successfully increased the efficiency or effectiveness of what you do by how you do it, the very next leg of your successful turnkey Management System is **orchestration,** by which we mean <u>documenting</u> the innovative improvement you've made on HOW you do WHAT you do, so that every individual in your team is able to MASTER the new, innovatively disruptive methodology, which has enabled you to produce greater, more effective results, time after time, after time.

Which is, of course, the very meaning of "turnkey":

The ability to replicate successful behavior. Again and again, without fail.

Because, to the degree that you're unable to replicate successful behavior, your ability to grow is not only hampered, but blocked. Keeping you in that unfortunate state most companies find themselves in, looking for better and better people in the hope that they will bring better and better results.

It's the people, most companies say.

If that were true, that success resides in finding better and better people, Ford Motor Company would have never succeeded.

Nor would it have grown.

No company can.

To the contrary, success—which means your ability to grow exponentially, effectively and predictably—resides not in the acquisition of better and better people, but in the creation of exemplary systems, which ordinary people with the minimum required skills and capability can learn to master. Continuously. Which is why I say that your company's ultimate success depends upon the creation of an exemplary turnkey Management System, which says, to all and sundry, "This is how we manage here!" And it does not depend upon your ability to find and hire exemplary managers, but upon your exemplary ability to systematize the management of your affairs.

Which would suggest that in an exemplary company, exemplary managers are made, not born. ✤

BECOMING BETTER THAN THE BEST YOU CAN BE

The most important figures that one needs for management are unknown or unknowable but successful management must nevertheless take account of them.

—W. Edwards Deming

Exemplary managers are made by the continuous improvement of your operating systems, the innovation, quantification, and orchestration of everything you do and how you do it, to produce the extraordinary results your company is committed to produce on behalf of your customers. Because when you accomplish that, you have accomplished the Sole Purpose for your company's existence: to find and keep customers better than your competition can and does.

But, taking into account the function of continuous improvement, it means the continuous improvement of your company's behavior and performance, beyond where it is today, and beyond anything you have ever imagined you could do before. Again and again, over and over, always, forever, and yet again!

Every Company a School

And this is why I say, to anyone who is willing to listen, that every company is a school.

A school for its most important students: the people it attracts, hires, inspires, teaches, trains, coaches, and mentors, to become masters at everything they are expected to do, from their first role as apprentice, to their next role as craftsman, to their next role as master of the preliminary assignment they're expected to fill. And then to the next, and the next, and the next assignment, an ever-increasingly more significant, more strategic role in the evolution of the Enterprise of which they are a part. Which says that in an exemplary company, an entrepreneurial exemplary company, of course, the expectation of everyone is that, just like the Enterprise they've joined—your company—they are expected to grow, and then to grow, and then to grow, from the first-level assignment, to the next higher assignment, and then to the next higher assignment following that.

Each and every accountability your people are assigned to fulfill is a step on the ladder of what I call *The Hierarchy of Growth*. And unless and until your people have committed themselves to this process of personal continuous improvement, to the evolution of their own, personal enterprise, the system for growth will simply become an empty mission, full of empty words, stripped of all the potency those words are meant to possess.

And so it follows that, similarly, should that be the case, your company will not possess the potency of meaning you intended for it to possess as you fashioned your Dream, your Vision, your Purpose, your Mission.

And all of these dynamics and promises reside in the heart of your turnkey Management System. And they will live, systemically, at the very fiber of everything your company commits itself to do.

So your turnkey Management System is a measure and a living statement of everything you intend to do, the way you intend to do it, the outcome it is intended to produce, and the continuous improvement of each and everything I just mentioned.

And each and every measurement is done in real time, not as a review of the past. Which means that the process of innovation, quantification, and orchestration is an active component of the operation of your company every day, in every way.

Which means that you (and all other stakeholders who rely on those measurements) know, every day, what your expectations are and how well you've achieved them, or where you've fallen short, and for what reason.

Your Turnkey Management System as Brand Enforcer

Ultimately, a manager's true accountability is to understand what your turnkey Management System is telling him or her; to listen to the feedback, know how to interpret the measures of the operation over expectations, know how to improve the operational integrity of your turnkey Practices (however many comprise the Business), and where the gaps are revealed, not only in each and every one of the Practices, but between each and every one of them. Because each and every one of your turnkey Practices is, in itself, an essential component of your turnkey Business Aggregate of Practices.

Those Practices demonstrate and represent the fundamental components of your Business—the visual, emotional, functional and financial components of your customers' experience of your turnkey Business Aggregate. Each of them should look, feel, work and produce capital in exactly the same way, and to exactly the same standard expected of each of them to honor what they are all there to represent: YOUR BRAND.

An Apple Store lives and breathes on behalf of the Apple Brand.

The Apple Store is an Apple Business, comprised of Apple Practices, each of which consist of intentional components of the operating reality of an Apple Store, from the Genius Bar to the arrangement and demonstration of Apple products throughout the store, to the lighting and layout and color palette—each of which is a sub-system, each of which is intelligently invented to fulfill the Apple Dream, Vision, Purpose, and Mission, as evoked, invented, and imagined by Apple's extreme Dreamer, Steve Jobs.

Which is who, I'm suggesting, you're to become.

The Steve Jobs of your industry.

Why not?

Do you choose it?

Are you ready?

It must be turnkey if it is to work.

And then you can finally, once and for all, step up to invent your ENTERPRISE. ♣

PART V

Part V: Chapter Nineteen

CLIMBING YOUR MOUNTAIN

We shall have no better conditions in the future if we are satisfied with all those which we have at present.

—Thomas Edison

It should not surprise you that in my lifetime of working with business owners, and meeting them in countless hotel lobbies after countless keynotes at a seemingly infinite number of industry association conferences, seminars, and workshops—spanning every continent of the planet—while so many of them have been inspiring, focused, determined entrepreneurs, I have also had the occasion to meet a disconcerting number of wholly unhappy owners of companies.

All of them dependably display an abject lack of inspiration, coupled with a willingness, even a need, to remain where they are, in their comfort zone. They're in that place they've arrived at, accepting only too willingly the material gains they've made as far as they've gone, with absolutely no interest in threatening the equilibrium (or instability) of the status of their physical and emotional efforts made up to this point.

And they all want to fight me. They want to argue with me. Reason with me. Challenge me. Call me out.

Like a boxer who's won a few, but still remains to fight in the lower divisions, getting his brains beat out, bearing the daily pain of it, but happy to have what little he's earned, displaying his bruises proudly; at least he's gotten this far and stayed in the game! You might call it a sort of pride of the valley; I've got my little house, and my little car, and a few bucks set aside for my old age, but, hey, don't show me the mountain, don't talk to me about the climb, don't tell me that the valley is where the comfort seekers settle down to live out their days, because I don't see many of those guys who climb the mountain ever coming back, do you? You are not going to persuade *me* to risk *that* trip, Gerber!

The Enterprise IS the mountain, dear climbers.

The Enterprise is what this entire thing has been all about.

Because if your Dream is a real Dream, not just a fantasy; and if your Vision is built upon solidly attainable, sure-as-certain bedrock; and if your Purpose is deeply steeped in meaning, a meaning that stimulates the higher mind and higher heart of you, then there are people out there for whom your work, your energy, your passion, your intelligence, your discipline, your will, and your absolute determination can deeply and fully and purposefully serve.

If all of what I just expressed is true (or can become true—should you choose to do the work necessary to make it so), then your Mission is charged with exactly the righteous energy needed to lead your stunning capability forward to be embraced everywhere the people you need and who need your Mission are to be found.

Welcome to your mountain.

We're almost to the end of our journey. ♣

Part V: Chapter Twenty

WHAT'S AN ENTERPRISE?

To venture causes anxiety, but not to venture is to lose one's self . . . And to venture in the highest is precisely to become conscious of one's self.

—Soren Kierkegaard

What is an enterprise?

What's the view from the top of that mountain?

An Enterprise is an aggregate of up to seven turnkey Businesses plus a turnkey Leadership System!

It's that simple!

It is easiest to see the simplicity of this hierarchy of growth—this progression from your Dream to your Job to your Enterprise—when you're at this mountainous elevation. Take in that classic 10,000-foot view, where the air is cleanest, thinnest, and sparkling with absolute clarity.

From this elevation, you can see, far below you, your one Practice, having evolved from a Job with the creation and implementation of your prototype turnkey Client Acquisition System. You can see and marvel at it doing what it does—fulfilling your Dream, Vision, Purpose, and Mission in a single operation, with the highest level of consistency.

If you zoom back a bit, you see the expansion of your Practice into a Business—a multiplicity of up to seven Practices, now each with its own, but identical, Client Fulfillment and Client Acquisition Systems, seamlessly coordinated by the addition of your turnkey Management System. This is the system that provides the Business with the constant loop of two-way communications, coordinating, overseeing, monitoring, mentoring, and directing the maintenance of "the way we do it here" consistently within and between your seven Practices. From this elevation, especially, you can see that Management System as the center hub around which its seven perfect Practices orbit; seven moons, balanced in their coordinated orbit by the constant charge and force of gravity supplied by your turnkey Management System.

And now here we are at the next level of magnitude, the top of the mountain: The Enterprise.

Remember: **An Enterprise is an aggregate of up to seven turnkey Businesses plus a turnkey Leadership System!**

From this elevation, hovering just above your mountaintop, you can see those seven Businesses in alignment because, as you could see one turnkey Business, you can see seven. Each one of them absolutely the same.

Because within each of them there exists seven turnkey Practices.

Each one of which is absolutely the same.

Because within each of those seven turnkey Practices there exists a Client Fulfillment System at the heart of it all. Seven of them, each and every one of which is absolutely the same.

So, here at the top of this mountain, you see that your Enterprise is the aggregate of <u>up to 49 turnkey Practices</u>, each one of them operating in accordance with all the turnkey systems which comprise them.

All managed, improved upon continuously through your turnkey Management System. Innovated, quantified, and orchestrated to a fare-thee-well!

And continuously improving.

See the simplicity of it.

See the beauty of it.

See the congruence of it.

See the predictability of it.

See the genius of it.

See the systemic harmony and clarity of it.

Which leaves us with only one last question to pursue and one remaining system to create and install.

What is a <u>turnkey Leadership System</u>? ♣

WHAT IS YOUR LEADERSHIP SYSTEM?

Your love has lifted me higher than I've ever been lifted before.

—Jackie Wilson

THE DNA OF YOUR ENTERPRISE

The DNA of your Enterprise—its genetic code, if you will—is formed by your imagination, which is the fuel for your inspiration, which is the energy residing at the very core of what your enterprise was intended to accomplish during its lifetime.

Try to picture it.

Imagine the action of mitosis taking place at that cellular level of your Dream. See how this hierarchy of growth manifests itself in each and every overarching progression toward the transparently obvious drive for expansion. Splitting, duplicating, combining. Splitting. Duplicating. Combining. The realization of the Dream, the Vision, the Purpose, and the Mission.

The visual template, the emotional template, the physical template, the financial template.

The unique code for every would-be Enterprise, without which, there is no way to frame its progress, to chart its evolution.

So, everything depends upon those very first steps taken so long ago.

The Dreaming is the essential driver of it all.

Without your Dreaming, to awaken and inspire your Vision, your Purpose, and your Mission, the heart of your journey would cease to beat and fail you when it was most needed.

Taking that first step, that absolutely necessary step, was actually your very first act of leadership. Without your leadership drive (whether you recognized it at the time or not), that first step would, at best, have remained small. At worst—not even leave a footprint.

TO LEAD IS TO INSPIRE

Leadership resides as the guiding force within every human being.

It might be said that we are born to lead. First ourselves, then our peers, then our family, then our community, then our world. Each of us possesses the possibility to lead ourselves, through the ascension of our aligned passions for living fully, creatively, imaginatively, inspirationally, spiritually, physically, mentally, and emotionally.

This is every human being's gift.

To inspire.

Unfortunately, few of us are taught this as children. It might be said that we are left to discover it on our own, or not. The signals we receive as children and then through adolescence are, at best, veiled instructions, brought to us in the form of edicts and directions, rather than inspiration.

Clean your room. Do your homework. Be a good girl or boy. Get good grades.

Of course these instructions are the product of other human beings' genuine efforts to exercise leadership (as, a generation earlier, they experienced it)—but, more often than not, are interpreted as a need to control, rather than inspire.

But the "true north" for the leader is <u>inspiration</u>.

I had a very successful entrepreneur/client who referred to his position in his Enterprise as the C.I.O.–the Chief Inspiration Officer!

One must inspire to lead.

And, to lead, one must *be* inspired.

And this purest manifestation of inspiration is not driven by some obligation to be "good," for gain or reward, but rather as a calling, invisible such as that might be. The calling to arise. The calling to live one's life fully. The calling to fulfill one's destiny. The calling to understand and fulfill the great abiding reason one has come to be on this planet.

To believe there is such a reason is the first sign of the leader within revealing itself. "There is a reason I am here," the leader says. So, the purpose of leadership is to fulfill that mission. One's life's mission.

THE VITALITY AT THE HEART OF YOUR LEADERSHIP SYSTEM

Nothing was more important to the vitality of Apple than the vitality which made it Apple, and which still makes it Apple today.

Nothing was more important to the vitality of Walmart than the vitality which made it Walmart, and which still makes it Walmart today.

Nothing is more important to the vitality of Nordstrom's than the vitality which made it Nordstrom's, and endures today.

Nothing is more important to the vitality of Zappos than the vitality which made it Zappos, and continues to inspire its enterprise today.

Nothing is more important to the vitality of 1-800-GOT-JUNK than the vitality of the founder's vision that continues to inspire its enterprise today.

The vitality at the core of your Enterprise that must be sustained with the very same vitality which both gave it birth back in the days when its Dream, Vision, Purpose, and Mission were being defined and described, as well as in those weeks, months and years in which that vitality took form as the living and thriving Enterprise it is today.

So it follows that the creation of your Dream, Vision, Purpose, and Mission cannot be taken lightly. For, if taken lightly, it will never survive the vicissitudes of growth, the earnest execution of the systems upon which your organization is dependent for its very survival, let alone its command of excellence.

THE PERSONAL REQUIREMENTS OF LEADERSHIP

As applied to your Enterprise, your Leadership System is, among other things, the methodology through which every member of your organization's team is likewise inspired to discover the leader in themselves. It is a system that, both directly and indirectly inspires, teaches, trains, coaches, models, and mentors those who choose to be on the path to become leaders.

The leader is a great Storyteller. She knows the story of the Enterprise she leads, and never tires of telling that story, not as a narcissistic balm to calm the concerns of her people, but as an inspiring revelation of the epiphanies such stories possess when told with the fire of authenticity.

The Story must be so deeply-rooted and authentic that everyone within the organization not only believes in it—in the grand tradition of it, in the sweat and tears and energy that went into bringing it to life and sustaining it—but can re-tell it themselves, bring themselves into the Story, add their own color and personal passion, and be deeply earnest in their pursuit of a greater understanding of how all of that came to pass. So much so that they are inspired to make it a part of their own story.

A great leader means to foretell. To foretell as a leader is to tell the story of a future one holds to be sacrosanct for the continued success of the Enterprise.

To foretell as an enterprise leader is somewhat akin to being a fortuneteller–but one who truly holds all the cards and *knows* the outcome! That's not trickery; it's a profound demonstration of informed and impassioned predictiveness!

Because to foretell calls for both an extreme understanding of the organization's evolution, the structure and capabilities which define its strengths as well as its weaknesses, the reality of the market for which it presumes to assume the preeminent role of leader, and how it will serve that market.

The leader is a sensitive observer of the flow of energy, both ascendant and descendent energies, the up and the down of it, the way every organization breathes in and breathes out, and the absolute certainty of it. There are moments in an organization's evolution in which leadership inspires great gusts of momentum, and moments in which leadership must reposition resources, direction, and the attention of each of the squads to better and more clearly define the way work is designed, built, launched, and grown.

The leader is always a great listener, both to messages actively sent her way, and to messages hiding as shadows in the workplace. But it's not just the messages themselves the leader listens for, but the messages within the messages; not the overt speaking, but the often covert speaking which spreads the disaffection with means and ends among people who, for whatever reason, have lost touch with the Enterprise's overriding *raison d'être* and, having done so, have become freewheeling spirits off on their own, neither here nor there, neither participating nor disassociating, but, in the words of transcendence, reeling.

The leader must always be aware of this.

And, once aware, provide the method for reversing this.

It's as though the very energy of the Enterprise has the power, not only to pull participants in, but to throw participants out, as well.

It's the Leadership System's role to reveal this.

It's the Leadership System that tells the leader what is what, where is where, and who is who.

It's the Leadership System's intelligence which enables the leader to translate activity of the Enterprise into signs of congruence or incongruence.

Signs of balance or signs of imbalance.

Signs of harmony or signs of disharmony.

Leadership Stands with Standards

In order for there to be harmony, balance, or congruence, there must be standards which define harmony, balance, and congruence.

Without standards, there can be no intelligence.

Without standards there can be no agreement or disagreement.

Without standards there can be no Management System or Leadership System.

Which takes us back all the way to the very beginning of this book and The Evolution of an Enterprise.

Indeed, without standards there can be no Dream, Vision, Purpose, or Mission.

At the heart of the heart, and from the very outset of every entrepreneurial organization whose watchword is "world class" or "excellent," must be Standards.

If you have none, nor will your Enterprise.

If you have none, nor will your Business.

If you have none, nor will your Practice.

If you have none, nor will your Job.

And if you have none, nor will your life, dear friend.

So, that's where I leave you.

Come join us to transform the state of your life through the intentional evolution of your Entrepreneurial Enterprise.

Become your own leader in a journey unlike any you have ever taken before. ✤

THE EPILOGUE

If something comes to life in others because of you, then you have made an approach to immortality.

—Norman Cousins

A great friend, and a serious business guy at the top of his game, suggested—quite strongly, in fact—that I discount my subtitle "From a Company of One to a Company of 1,000!" to a Company of perhaps 10 or certainly no more than 100.

Suggesting, as he did, that my reader, you, would be totally put off by a Company of 1,000!

That very few small business owners are even willing to think 1,000!

That the very thought of 1,000 would shut you down.

That upon seeing 1,000, you wouldn't even open the book!

I disagreed with him.

Because, in the long run, it wasn't you I was telling to grow your company to 1,000, it was that guy who is going to buy your company.

But, if you didn't prepare your company to scale, to grow, and to possess the capability, the capacity, the systems, to be able to grow to 1,000, and even beyond, who in the world would buy it?

It certainly would not be someone with the capital and the passion to grow a major enterprise.

And if your buyer wasn't someone with the capital and the passion to grow a major enterprise, why would we go to all this trouble?

Well, of course, we wouldn't.

And now we're done.

The shortest book I've ever written (with, admittedly, quite possibly, the longest subtitle).

The last of my E-Myth books; the third and final one in my *E-Myth Trilogy*.

The first is *The E-Myth Revisited*.

The second is *Awakening the Entrepreneur Within*.

And this is the third: *Beyond The E-Myth*.

I suppose that when you get right down to it, I could have selected every one of my E-Myth books and created a boxed set out of all of them, but having completed this book, I didn't think it should be necessary.

Because in this book, I think we nailed it down tight.

The paradigm I have called *The E-Myth* is now complete and ready for you to actually implement it.

Which means that if you have never actually done what I laid out in my previous books, have never actually turn-keyed your company to the degree I've described, in this book I've spelled it out so exactly, so clearly, so emphatically, that now you can implement it and, by so doing, design, build, launch, and grow your spectacular company to scale.

This means, to grow.

Which means, to get it prepared for sale.

You can do this.

Are you ready?

We are ready to help.

Taking the Next Step to Grow

We've built the process for guiding you step-by-step from a "Company of One" to wherever you wish to go.

We call it **Beyond The E-Myth: The Program.**

To find out more, simply email us at Gerber@MichaelEGerber.com

We'll tell you about our Dreaming Room, led by a brilliantly prepared Dreaming Room Leader, who will take you through the process of building your platform for growth, setting the foundation for what we've consolidated here in *Beyond The E-Myth,* by uncovering your Dream, your Vision, your Purpose, and your Mission.

And then to implement it all in the evolution of your Enterprise.

To actually do exactly what I've laid out for you in this book.

No matter how small your company is today, or how large.

The process is in place to turn what you might dismiss as an academic exercise into the most pragmatic, intentional, and dynamic application it was always designed to be.

And that's why I say, dear friend, come dream with me.

Come build a worldwide Enterprise.

Let's put into practice what I've spent my life getting ready to do, to transform the state of small business worldwide, by creating the transferable system which can be applied to every small company, and to prove to you, once and for all, that every small business is a school and that every life is a legacy.

Let's speak soon.

Warmly,

Michael E. Gerber
Chairman and Co-Founder
Chief Dreamer
Michael E. Gerber Companies, Inc.™

ABOUT THE AUTHOR
Michael E. Gerber

Innovator, Entrepreneur, Author, and Thought Leader . . .

Everyone who knows small business knows Michael E. Gerber.

- The Bestselling author of 29 'E-Myth' books, in *The New York Times, The Wall Street Journal, Business Week, Inc. Magazine, FORTUNE, Forbes, Wired* . . . millions sold;

- Translated in more than 29 languages and used today as the entrepreneur text in over 118 universities;

- The originator, in 1977, of the small business coaching industry, with his founding of The Michael Thomas Corporation, The E-Myth Academy, E-Myth Worldwide, Michael E. Gerber Companies, Inc.™ . . . since that time having served over 100,000 small business clients in 145 countries;

- The Creator of the entrepreneurial incubator called, The NEW Dreaming Room now being delivered worldwide, an intense, innovative 2½-day intensive for new, and awakening, entrepreneurs; and

- Today launching *"Beyond The E-Myth–The Evolution of an Enterprise: From a Company of One to a a Company of 1,000!: The Course–The Program"*–a revolutionary process to prepare a small company for acquisition by readying it to scale. **"Scale to Sale!™"**

Michael E. Gerber states, ***"Every Life a Legacy!–Every Small Business a School!"*** His work with small business owners around the world has led to the transformation of tens of thousands of small companies, and the creation of a platform for intelligent, managed, socially profound growth.

His "Dream": **"To Transform the state of small business worldwide."**

ABOUT THE E-MYTH TRILOGY

The *E-Myth Trilogy* brings Michael E. Gerber's proven E-Myth philosophy to a wide variety of different professional practice areas. The E-Myth, short for "Entrepreneurial Myth," is simple: too many small businesses fail to grow because their leaders think like technicians, not entrepreneurs. Gerber's approach gives small enterprise leaders practical, proven methods that have already helped transform more than 70,000 businesses. Let the Trilogy series boost your professional practice today!

Books in the Trilogy include:

- *The E-Myth Revisited*
- *Awaking the Entrepreneur Within*
- *Beyond The E-Myth*

Learn more at: **www.beyondemyth.com/trilogy**

Have you created an E-Myth enterprise? Would you like to become a co-author of an E-Myth book in your industry? Go to: **www.beyondemyth.com/co-author**

THE MICHAEL E. GERBER
ENTREPRENEUR'S LIBRARY
It Keeps Growing...

Thank you for reading **Beyond The E-Myth.**

We, at Michael E. Gerber Companies, are determined to
Realize the Dream Gerber Intended in 1977:
"To transform the state of small business and
entrepreneurship worldwide!"

To find out more, email us at:
Gerber@MichaelEGerber.com.

To find out how YOU can apply the E-Myth to YOUR Company of One,
email us at:
Gerber@MichaelEGerber.com.

Thank you for living your Dream, changing your
focus, and creating a New, Robust World

Michael E. Gerber, Co-Founder/Chairman
Michael E. Gerber Companies™
Creator of The E-Myth Evolution™
P.O. Box 130384, Carlsbad, CA 92013
760-752-1812 O • 760-752-9926 F
Gerber@MichaelEGerber.com
www.michaelegerbercompanies.com

JOIN THE EVOLUTION^{SM}

Find the latest updates:
www.michaelegerbercompanies.com

Attend The Dreaming Room™ Trainings
www.michaelegerbercompanies.com

Watch the latest videos
www.youtube.com/michaelegerber

Connect on LinkedIn
www.linkedin.com/in/michaelegerber

Connect on Facebook
www.facebook.com/MichaelEGerberCo

Follow on Twitter
http://twitter.com/michaelegerber